CLARKES CAFE

REDACRE ROAD

SHOPS
CORNER OF
BOLDMERE ROAD
AND REDACRE ROAD

Shops, corner of Boldmere Road and Redacre Road.

A HISTORY OF BOLDMERE

by
K. J. Williams

The Boldmere Boys Brass Band, circa 1900.

Westwood Press Publications

44 BOLDMERE ROAD, SUTTON COLDFIELD
WEST MIDLANDS B73 5TD
TELEPHONE: 0121-354 5913

Shop on corner of Jockey Road and Stonehouse Road around the 1920s

Acknowledgments

To Sutton Coldfield Reference Library for their excellent records without which it would have been impossible to write this history.

To Sutton Coldfield Local History Group whose members provided me with useful information.

To Dennis Hurley and Roger Lea for their encouragement and assistance in sorting out much required directories. To Norman V. Evans for his advice. To Miss Doreen Ogden for her Stonehouse Farm photographs and Boldmere memories and to Mr Bird of W. J. Bird & Son for his family bakery reminiscences.

The publisher would also like to thank all those members of the Boldmere Traders Association who provided additional information and illustrations to help enhance this book.
Reg Hollins, Westwood Press Publications

© Copyright Westwood Press
First Edition Autumn 1994

Printed & Published by The Westwood Press, 44 Boldmere Road Sutton Coldfield, West Midlands. Produced by Offset Litho.

Contents

PART ONE

PART TWO

CASSON — Ladies Fashion Shoes, Hats and Accessories
18 Boldmere Road · Sutton Coldfield · 0121-355 6102

CORK AND BOTTLE
363-365 Boldmere Road · Boldmere · Sutton Coldfield · 0121-382 4430

FLEETWOOD DELICATESSEN — Delicatessen & Bakery
51-53 Boldmere Road · Sutton Coldfield · 0121-354 1898

JOHN FROST LTD — Dispensing Chemists
80-82 Boldmere Road · Sutton Coldfield · 0121-354 2121

GABY TRAVEL ABTA 31032 IATA 91-2-91491
20 Boldmere Road · Sutton Coldfield · B73 5TD · Tel 0121-354 4444 · Fax 0121-355 6996

P A GANNOD (GANNONS) — Hairdresser
249 Jockey Road · Boldmere · Sutton Coldfield · 0121-354 8383

THE HEALTH STORE — Retailer Health Foods & Supplements
26 Boldmere Road · Sutton Coldfield · B73 5TD

K P HEARNE F.B.C.O. — Ophthalmic Optician
66 Boldmere Road · Sutton Coldfield · B73 5TJ · 0121-354 6411

J T H JONES & SON — Plumbers & Heating Engineers (CORGI Registered)
257 Jockey Road · Sutton Coldfield · 0121-354 3242

H KEENAN LIMITED — Monumental Stonemasons
185-187 Boldmere Road · Sutton Coldfield · B73 5UL · 0121-354 6144

KILROY & CO — Solicitors
333 Jockey Road · Boldmere · Sutton Coldfield · B73 5XE · 0121-354 5227

MERE TRIMMINGS — Furnishing Trimmings
24 Boldmere Road · Sutton Coldfield · B73 5TD · 0121-321 2522

MIDLAND BANK PLC — Bankers
90 Boldmere Road · Sutton Coldfield · B73 5UA · 0121-354 8116

MISCELLANY — Pine & Cane Furniture, Gifts of All Types
98 Boldmere Road · Sutton Coldfield · 0121-355 6806

ONE JUMP AHEAD — Pine, Country Furniture, Pictures, Mirrors
60B Boldmere Road · Sutton Coldfield · B73 5TJ · 0121-355 7280

PETER'S 1931 VINTAGE WEDDING ROLLS-ROYCE — Wedding Car
9 Redacre Road · Boldmere · Sutton Coldfield · 0121-354 6615

W POWELL & SON —High Class Family Butchers
86 Boldmere Road · Sutton Coldfield · B73 5TJ · 0121-354 2721

PRIVATE COLLECTION '86 — Gifts · Mirrors · Pictures · Gifts · Pine · Soft Furnishing
60 Boldmere Road · Sutton Coldfield · B73 5TJ · 0121-354 3599

POWELECTRICS LIMITED — Electrical Distributors
Concorde House · Union Drive · off Boldmere Road · Sutton Coldfield · B73 5TE · 0121-354 7877

REMAINDERS LTD (T/A THE WORKS) — Booksellers
Head Office · 13-19 Gate Lane · Boldmere · Sutton Coldfield · B73 5TR

RYDALE-SUTTON — BMW Dealer (Motor Trade)
Jockey Road · Boldmere · Sutton Coldfield · 0121-354 8131

St CATHERINES RESIDENTIAL HOME — Home for the Elderly
328 Boldmere Road · Sutton Coldfield · B73 5EU · 0121-377 8178

D SINE — Padlock Manufacturers
5-7 Gate Lane · Boldmere Road · Sutton Coldfield · B73 5TR · 0121-354 3875

TREVOR SHORT'S GOLF SHOP — Retail Golf Shop
Monmouth Drive · Sutton Coldfield · 0121-354 3379

SINGULAR SENSATION — Bridalwear
8 Boldmere Road · Sutton Coldfield · B73 5TD · 0121-355 8158

J F SOCCI & CO — Chartered Accountants
61 Boldmere Road · Sutton Coldfield · B73 5XA · 0121-321 2116

SUTTON KITCHENS — International Kitchen Designers
41 Boldmere Road · Sutton Coldfield · B73 5UY · 0121-355 1101

THOMAS & JONES — Jewellers, Watch & Clock Repairers
56 Boldmere Road · Sutton Coldfield · B73 5TJ · 0121-354 7298

TSB BANK PLC — Bank
76 Boldmere Road · Sutton Coldfield · B73 5TJ · 0121-354 6856

VOGUE OF BOLDMERE — Ladies Fashion Retailer
57-59 Boldmere Road · Sutton Coldfield · 0121-354 6622

WATERLOO HOUSING ASSOCIATION LTD — Housing Association
Waterloo House · 76/78 Boldmere Road · Sutton Coldfield · B73 5TJ · 0121-355 4651

WELLWORTH PET CARE
92a Boldmere Road · Sutton Coldfield · B73 5UB · 0121-355 2078

WESTWOOD PRESS — Printers and Publishers
44 Boldmere Road · Sutton Coldfield · B73 5TD · 0121-354 5913

PUBLISHERS NOTICE

Whilst every care has been taken to verify dates and events herein the untimely death of the author meant we had no source to refer to. We therefore apologise if any errors of fact have been made.

Preface

The study of local history, the formation of local history societies and groups whether for research or purely interest has expanded enormously since the end of the 1939-45 War.

Whereas previously it was most difficult to find a history of a small town, village or district of a large city, today local historians have put pen to paper and there is a whole wealth of books to be found on such subjects throughout most regions of the country.

I hope my contribution *A History of Boldmere* will give as much pleasure to the reader as it gave to me whilst I was writing it.

New Oscott 1993   *K. J. Williams*

About the Author

Ken Williams died at the end of 1993, having put the finishing touches to *A History of Boldmere* from his sick-bed. His other work in progress was a video guide to the history of Sutton Park, of which volume one has been issued, as a successor to his video *A Walk through Old Sutton Town*. This interest in seeing history through pictures is reflected in the many original drawings by Ken which are included in this book.

After 35 years working for Ty-Phoo Tea, Ken retired in 1987 and devoted more time and energy to his interest in local history, which had already resulted in a mass of unpublished work on the mills of Sutton Coldfield, and his *History of New Oscott* (privately published) in 1985. His article, *Langley Water Mill* was published in *Scenes from Sutton's Past* (Westwood Press 1989), and *The Story of Ty-Phoo and the Birmingham Tea Industry* came out in 1990. He was a founder of the Sutton Coldfield Local History Research Group, and well-known to other local groups as a speaker on local history topics.

Part of Speed's Map of Warwickshire, 1610.

A History of Boldmere

PART 1

Boldmere Landmarks

At the time of Bishop Vesey's Sutton in 1527, Boldmere as a district did not yet exist, the area being an open, wild and windy expanse, covered with gorse.

Speed's map of 1610 aptly names the area as *Cofeld Wast* which subsequently became known as *The Coldfield* and later, in the 19th century, as *Boldmere*, through its proximity to Baldmoor Lake on Chester Road. A writer in 1679 refers to "some land about this spot is described as being between Sutton Park, the land then or late of John Allport, and the common called *The Coldfield*".

The district of Boldmere is of triangular shape being within the confines of Chester Road, Jockey Road and Boldmere Road, with slight overlaps. It is bounded by Sutton Park, Wylde Green, New Oscott and Erdington.

Farms

The Earliest Settlements Consisted of 3 Farms and the Spade Mill

Some of the earliest settlements in the *Coldfield* consisted of three farms adjacent to the park boundary, the line of which in 1527 is described today, approximately, by Monmouth Drive. The farms consisting of *Old Park Farm* situated near the present New Oscott School, Markham Road; *Booths Farm*, approximately at the junction of Darnick Road and Halton Road; and finally *Stonehouse Farm*, the site of the farmhouse being now occupied by a bungalow on the corner of Stonehouse Road and Corbridge Road.

Cattle from the farms were able to graze on the slopes of the *Coldfield* and drink water from the small stream rising at Longmoor in the park, which made its way unimpeded through the valley now covered by the waters of *Powell's Pool*. Both *Longmoor* and *Powell's Pool* dams were of 18th century origin, and at the time of Vesey the area of Powell's was within the park, but later found itself outside through various 16th century encroachments. It came back into the park in 1937 when acquired by the Corporation.

1856 Valuation Map

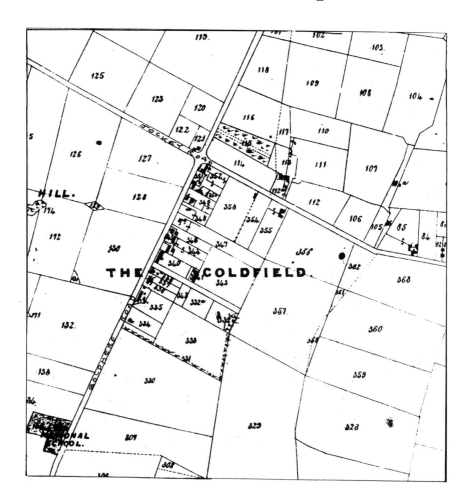

Every field and house was surveyed and valued, in order to establish new parishes such as St Michael's Boldmere. No. 334 is Grove Cottage, at the time the last house in Boldmere. This is the last of three maps at this scale, the first two being made in connection with the enclosures of the commons; on these maps, most of the section shown here was a blank. The roads were drawn in with a ruler, and then fields of various sizes ruled off for allotments to the various people entitled to land. Many of the rectangles and angles are preserved in the modern street pattern.

Stonehouse Farm, Boldmere   KJWilliams
                                                1990

Stonehouse Farm

Tom Porter, who was Sutton's Borough Surveyor and Engineer, drew attention to the antiquity of *Stonehouse Farm* in the 1965 publication *Sutton Park, a History and Guide,* when he wrote:

> *"I have noticed when the pool is lowered that there is a road running diagonally from the golf course side to the other, and I assume it was an access road running from Stonehouse Farm to the meadows on the other side of the pool, long before the water was impounded".*

Conditions at *Stonehouse Farm* remained considerably primitive until the early 1900s. This was confirmed in a report by the Park and Estates Committee in 1913, which stated that *Stonehouse Farm* was entirely without water, being then not connected to the water mains.

Water for domestic use was obtained from a hand cranked water pump situated near the side door of the farmhouse. The water pump survived until the 1950s and appears on a photograph taken just prior to the demolition of the farmhouse.

In 1864 Samuel Frederick Fellows was tenant farmer and by 1890 George Austin Cooper was in occupation. From about 1896 until the mid 1900s, the Fellows family were again running the farm, when in the 1950s it ceased as a farm and the buildings were demolished.

Tenant farmer of nearby *Old Park Farm* from about 1824 until the 1850s was George Cooper, with the proprietor being William Spurrier. The census of 1841 shows George Cooper aged 50, his wife Mary also 50, son George 25, daughters Mary 20 and Frances 15. It was probably son George who in 1890 was the farmer at *Stonehouse Farm.*

A photograph in the possession of Mrs Doreen Ogden shows *Stonehouse Dairy Farm,* this was exactly opposite her bungalow in Stonehouse Road, which was built in one of Fellows' fields.

She remembers as a child seeing cattle from the farm being driven down the path alongside her bungalow to be turned out into the fields beyond, long before Monmouth Drive was laid.

Miss Ogden recalled that Mr Fellows had three sons, the eldest being Charles and the youngest Fred. To the right of the farm was a labourer's cottage occupied by Mr and Mrs Bayliss and their farm labourer son, Arthur, who appears in the photograph standing at the entrance to the farm.

Arthur was the cowman and responsible for taking the cows to the fields twice a day.

She recalls how she and other local children would be delighted when once a year the threshing machine arrived at the farm and was put to work. The bottom of her garden was where Mr Fellows used to keep his poultry and beyond that were the wheat and cereal fields where she used to go blackberrying and have picnics.

After the 1939-1945 War the Fellows family left the farm and a family called Buchanan came and lived there for a few years before the farmhouse was pulled down.

Stonehouse Farm/Fellows Farm, 49 Stonehouse Road, photograph taken in the 1920s. The cowman Arthur Bayliss is pictured.

Booths Farm

Records in existence show that at *Booths Farm* from 1834 until the late 1870s the Buggins family were in occupation with the farm passing from father to son. From the early 1880s until 1928, the Plant family were running the farm. In 1928 the Bonell Family took over and remained there till the early 1950s when it was redeveloped for housing. John Buggins testified at an inquiry in 1855, when he was asked why such a substantial inhabitant had not been invited to join the Corporation, and whether he thought his Roman Catholicism had prevented it. His reply was non-committal, but his enterprise is shown by his early listing as a coal merchant.

It is interesting to note that in 1839 John Buggins sold a plot of ground in Boldmere for the erection of the original Roman Catholic Church.

The census of 1841 reveals that John Buggins and his wife, Hannah, both aged 45, were in occupation and then lists nine children with ages ranging from 5 years to 20 years, six of whom were girls and three being boys.

Spade Mill

A dramatic change to the landscape occurred in 1730 when Sir Alfred Holte erected a dam across the valley below *Stonehouse Farm*, thus covering 48 acres with water to create the largest pool in Sutton Coldfield, which is today called *Powell's Pool*. This effectively impeded access to the park from the three farms. From then on the nearest entrance would be across the stream below the dam in Park Lane, later called Stonehouse Road, and through what is now Boldmere Gate.

Three years later in 1733 the rural tranquility of the area was to be disturbed by industrial activity when John Wyatt, an inventor and native of the town, set up an experimental cotton spinning machine in a small shed below the dam and utilised the waters of the pool to power it.

He described how in 1733 he shut himself up in a small building near Sutton Coldfield with his little machine, which was about two feet square and which he had invented:

> *"And there, in solitude and all the time me in a pleasant but trembling suspense, was spun the first thread of cotton yarn ever produced by mechanical means".*

The cotton had been carded in the usual way and was passed between two cylinders from whence the bobbin drew it by means of a twist.

Dogged by financial problems his progress was hindered and he failed to patent the invention. His ideas were taken up by others and in 1740 Lewis Paul, from whom Wyatt had borrowed money, entered into partnership with Lewis Cave (founder of *Gentlemen's Magazine*) and used a new device which had 100 spindles "to spin wool or cotton into thread or worsted".

It was left to Richard Arkwright, who patented his *Spinning Jenny* in 1769, incorporating rollers as key parts said to have been invented in 1738 by Lewis Paul, Wyatt's partner at *Powell's Pool*. Arkwright, a better manager, became financially successful, eventually receiving a Knighthood.

Beset by money troubles Wyatt moved to Birmingham using donkey power to spin cotton. In the Birmingham Museum, a hank of cotton produced by Wyatt in 1741 is on display.

He unfortunately ended up in a debtors' prison and died a pauper in 1766. He is buried in St Philip's Churchyard, Colmore Row, Birmingham.

From the small shed on the dam at *Powell's Pool*, Boldmere, Sutton Coldfield, the seeds of the industrial revolution were sown.

THE ROLLING MILL

By the 1750s a more substantial building had been erected below the dam worked by William Powell as a rolling mill. It is from William Powell the pool acquired its name, although over the years it has been variously called *Rolling Mill Pool*, *New Forge Pool*, before finally settling as *Powell's Pool*.

The Old Spade Mill, Stonehouse Road.

16

The Old Spade Mill from Powells Pool.

Carts carrying raw material and finished goods to and from the mill would negotiate the slope of Park Lane (Stonehouse Road) to gain access to Jockey Lane, and so to either Sutton Town or Chester Road and Birmingham or along what was a track, later called Boldmere Road, to Erdington and beyond.

SPADE MANUFACTURING STARTED

At some time during the 1830s Francis Parkes settled in the district and took over the mill. It then changed from a rolling mill to that of manufacturing spades. Consequently, a tilt hammer was installed to shape the metal. The Parkes family were involved with *Spade Mill* for over forty years, during which time several other people were associated with them in running the business, although ownership of the property was vested in Lord Somerville.

During the course of their tenancy the mill was responsible for turning out spades, garden forks, shovels and saws. In addition it provided employment for many local families. In 1855 upwards of 30 men and boys were employed there and the thump of the tilt hammer could be heard working throughout the night turning out agricultural tools, many of which were exported to the Commonwealth.

In 1882 rolling machinery was again being used at the mill and in 1904 Midgley in his book *Sutton Coldfield Town and Chase* recorded the mill was rolling steel for the Birmingham pen trade.

Millstones forming two steps at Powells Pool   *Waterwheel and Tilt Hammer for manufacturing spades, shovels, axes and blade tools.*

Since its creation in 1730 *Powell's Pool* had not only been a source of power to work a watermill, but also an amenity for the enjoyment of the local population, providing fishing, swimming, boating and, during winter, ice skating. In the 1880s the steamboat *Foam* became a feature of the pool, providing trips for the general public.

For many years *Boldmere Swimming Club* regularly used the pool for their events and galas and used the derelict mill as dressing rooms — it had earth floors.

Powell's Pool in 1990 with La Reserve in background.

When the 1914-18 War broke out the mill, which had been empty for some years, was put to work by the firm of John E. Mapplebeck in turning out brass strip for the war effort. Owner of the firm, Richard Brosch, and his two sons John and Leo travelled each day from their home on the corner of Chester Road and College Road, New Oscott, to work the mill.

A tragedy occurred at the mill in 1918 when William Harrison, a 39 year old local builder, was accidentally killed by the water-wheel. He had entered the mill alone and whilst attempting to start the water-wheel slipped and was crushed. The inquest returned a verdict of accidental death. He is buried in St Michael's Churchyard, Boldmere, an anchor clearly identifies his grave.

In 1936, the then derelict and empty mill, being in a dangerous condition, was demolished revealing its unusual pitch back water-wheel. The area was landscaped and today a water-fall tumbles over the rocks where once the water-wheel used to operate.

The grave of William Harrison, a builder, accidentally killed by the water-wheel of the Spade Mill in 1918.

18th Century Boldmere

Travel on the roads during the 18th century was fraught with danger, it being a time when highway robbery had reached its peak. For the lone traveller the vicinity of the *Coldfield* was particularly vulnerable should he venture that way.

William Twamley writing in 1855 draws attention to one unfortunate victim:

"There was buried on the 28th day of March 1729 John Johnson, a silk dyer from London, who was murdered upon Sutton Coldfield Common in this Parish (the common land then lying open, and for many years afterwards remained so).

Suspicion fell on a man named Edward Allport, as having committed the barbarous deed, who was a person of loose habits and bore a very indifferent character, whose house of rendezvous and place of resort (principally) was a small pot-house called or known by the Boot and Shoe on the left hand side of the Chester Road, near to the village of Erdington, by no means anything like a house of respectability but noted for women of bad character being kept at it".

Gibbet Hill

Allport was apprehended, tried and found guilty and was hung on a gibbet on what became known as *Gibbet Hill*, a prominence overlooking Boldmere behind the *New Oscott Tavern*. His body hung on the gibbet for a considerable time as a warning to others.

In 1742 another highwayman named Sansbury was caught with an accomplice when drunk and asleep in a cornfield. He was also hanged.

Around that time, Henry Hunt, a Birmingham man travelling along Chester Road, was accosted by two highwaymen and robbed of his watch and money.

William Hutton, the Birmingham Historian, visited Sutton in February 1783 and encountered problems trying to climb the hill overlooking the *Coldfield*, which he described as a hill of some magnitude, and whilst doing so found himself in the middle of a morass and had to retreat. He also recorded the name of the pool from which Boldmere was eventually to take its name:

> *"Upon the north-west extremity of Sutton Coldfield joining the Chester Road is the* Bowen Pool.*"*

By 1802 the name of the pool had changed and on the Erdington enclosure map was shown as *Bowmore Lake* and was divided by Chester Road. A further eight years on, in 1810, the name of the pool appears as *Baldmoor* and in 1848 as *Baldmoor Lake*.

In 1885 a Mr William Fowler said that in his younger days it was always spoken of as *Baldmoor*, commonly pronounced *Bolmer*.

Lakehouse Road built on the site of Baldmoor Lake which spanned the Chester Road. The Ecclesiastical Parish of Boldmere took its name from the lake.
photo: K. J. Williams 1990

Although the lake is no longer in existence, its dried bed being covered by a housing estate, it is commemorated by Lakehouse Road adjoining Chester Road.

St Nicholas R.C. Chapel — built 1840

The *Coldfield* in 1824 was still open common, there being no buildings in the vicinity other than three farms and a water-mill. Following the enclosure of the commons in 1825 owners were in a position to profit from their newly acquired land. Being previously uncultivated, a considerable amount of labour was required to bring the land into a productive state, and many of the labourers employed came to Sutton from elsewhere, a good proportion of them being from Ireland.

John Buggins, a local farmer, became the possessor of a plot of land on the corner of Boldmere Road and Jockey Lane, on part of which the *Sutton Park Hotel* now stands. On the 17th June 1839 he sold to the authorities of the Roman Catholic Church

> *"all that piece or parcel of land containing one rood and twenty-eight perches fronting the road there leading from Erdington or towards Sutton Park"*

(Boldmere Road then not yet having acquired its name).

St Nicholas RC Chapel and Old Cottages, Boldmere. Built 1840 and demolished 1961. There is a commemorative plaque on the wall of Lloyds Bank which now occupies the site.

On this land in 1840, was built by Bishop Wiseman, St Nicholas' Roman Catholic Chapel and adjoining cottages. Both the Chapel and the cottages were built to the plans of Augustus Welby Pugin and were among the first to be erected in Boldmere, thereby setting the trend for others to follow.

For the next thirty years the Chapel, seating fifty people, served the needs of the tiny scattered congregation, the services being conducted by the Clergy from Oscott College, New Oscott, which had been built in 1838.

A DISPUTE CLOSED THE CHAPEL FOR 13 YEARS

The Chapel closed in 1870 and remained closed for the next thirteen years through an internal dispute. The Chapel, not having been consecrated, was used as a storeroom and even kennels.

Mrs Plant of nearby *Booth's Farm* pestered the authorities until in 1883 she persuaded them to re-open it as a place of worship, the High Mass being sung by one of the Benedictine Fathers from Erdington Abbey. The monks were associated with the Chapel until 1922. The Chapel also incorporated a school. Behind the building was a burial ground.

The Jockey Road, Boldmere Road junction before the 1960s re-development — note the old R. C. Chapel is still standing on the left.

This picture shows the Grandparents of Mrs I. Ducker, standing in front of the Old Cottages. Her grandfather used the loft at the rear for shoe making and employing up to two men. Mrs Ducker says "The ladies of the day used to arrive in their carriages and crinolines to be measured for their boots. Sometimes grandfather would put on his Sunday best to visit the houses of the local gentry for the same purpose.

By 1929 the Chapel was too small and a scheme was set up and implemented, resulting, in the Autumn of 1929, in the erection of a new temporary Church at a cost of £1,600, which incorporated a sliding screen, allowing one part to be used for social purposes. The new Church was designed to accommodate 250 people.

In 1931, land in Jockey Road, adjacent to the Church Hall, was for sale consisting of two acres, including a detatched house, all of which was acquired for £2,000.

On March 10th 1953 a new Church was opened by Archbishop Masterson, although it was not until 1958 that the final addition was completed.

In 1968 the erection of St Nicholas School adjoining the new church was satisfactorily finished.

The old Chapel and cottages had been empty and derelict for a number of years, being the haven for sparrows and other birds and the target of vandals. They were sold and demolished in 1961 and a row of shops built on the site.

Behind the Chapel was a cemetery and the remains of those buried there were removed and re-interred at New Oscott College Cemetery. A plaque affixed to the front wall of Lloyds Bank, Boldmere commemorates the old St Nicholas Chapel.

Inns and Taverns

Beggars Bush Inn

Not far from St Nicholas Chapel, at the top of Jockey Lane, is "The Beggars Bush", where legend has it that a tramp or beggar was found dead under a hawthorn bush, which marked the boundary of Staffordshire and Warwickshire. An argument ensued between the two authorities as to who should pay the burial costs, but eventually they decided to share the expense.

It is not surprising, therefore, that at the busy crossroads marked by the bush, an inn should be built, appropriately named the *Bush Inn*, it being the first of three to be built on the site. It lay well back from the main Chester Road and was approached by one path leading from Chester Road and another from Jockey Lane and would have been in line with where the present bus stop at the top of Jockey Road now is.

The earliest record of a landlord at the inn is 1841, when William Goodwin aged 35 was listed in the census returns together with his 40 year old wife Mary, and their six children: William 15, George 10, Joseph 8, Sarah 4, Thomas 2 and Julia 1.

*Jockey Road running up towards the Beggars Bush Inn
in the early nineteen hundreds.*

In 1861 a new and larger *Beggars Bush Inn* was erected by William Goodwin on the corner of Jockey Lane and fronting Chester Road. He also built five cottages alongside, three of which were called *Holly Cottages*.

Within three months of having built the new *Beggars Bush Inn*, he was obliged to convert the old original *Bush Inn* into three cottages, having previously transferred the licence and signs on completion of the new building.

William Goodwin leased the inn and land from the Reverend W. K. Riland Bedford for a term of ninety-nine years, at an annual rent of £40.00

This second inn served its purpose until the 1930s when the present *Beggars Bush Inn* was built on land between the 1841 and 1861 buildings. When the new building was completed, the old 1861 inn was demolished, revealing the more modern and even larger hostelry which is still with us, having undergone in 1991 a major refurbishment.

The three cottages which were once the 1841 *Bush Inn* survived until the 1960s when they were demolished.

The Sutton Park Inn and The Gate Inn

By 1857 two inns along Boldmere Road had been established to meet passing and local trade. They were the *Sutton Park Inn*, and *Gate Inn*, on the corner of Gate Lane and Boldmere Road.

The Sutton Park Inn.

THE SUTTON PARK INN

The earliest record for the *Sutton Park Inn* is 1866 when Joseph Atkins was its proprietor. The next time a name crops up is in 1866 when Arthur Bezant is named. It is also in 1866 when we see that the name has changed to the *Sutton Park Tavern*, when another tenant, Arthur Plant, is named. From 1890 untill 1896 Richard Osman was the publican.

Since then the old inn has been demolished and the present *Sutton Park Hotel* built. The inn provided a service for the local population in providing rooms to let for various functions and for many years the Boldmere Swimming Club held their meetings there.

The Sutton Park Hotel which replaced the Sutton Park Inn

THE GATE INN

The *Gate Inn* was rather a quaint place with a five-barred gate suspended in front instead of a painted sign. In 1864 Samuel Lambert is recorded as the publican. By 1886 Henry Mee Junior was in charge. A succession of publicans followed until 1939 when the inn was demolished and in its place the *Boldmere Hotel* was erected. Today it is known as *The Harvester*.

Regularly advertised in local publications, the *Gate Inn* was in 1890 described as near Wylde Green Railway Station and within easy driving distance of Birmingham, West Bromwich, Walsall and adjacent towns and within five minutes walk of the Boldmere entrance to Sutton Park. They advertised every accommodation for public and private parties, and were district agents for Messrs Ansell & Sons, the licensee being Henry Mee and Sons.

The Gate Inn, demolished 1938. The Boldmere Hotel replaced it (now renamed the Harvester).

The Gate Inn, Football Team played in a field opposite. The gentleman in the bowler hat was the licensee. The centre forward was Herbert Morris, son of the station-master at Wylde Green. The third man from the right standing at the back was team secretary and grandfather of Mrs I. Ducker of D. Sine who supplied this photograph taken in the early 1900s.

Beer Retailers and Public Houses

In 1848 William Coley was shown in the *Sutton Coldfield Rates Book* to be the owner of a beer house on the *Coldfield*, and again in 1850 when his name was spelt Coaley. The early directories and rate books, whilst recording the names of various traders on the *Coldfield*, could not pinpoint the relevant properties as they were not yet numbered. Beer retailer is a trade description, but is not helpful in identifying the premises, whether it be an inn or private retail shop.

It may have been that some of the beer retailers recorded were situated at the Erdington end of Boldmere Road, where a cluster of small retail shops were built. In 1892 there was John Gwillam and a few years later in 1896 there was William Price. Between 1904 and 1912 Charles Dugmore, beer retailer, greengrocer and grocer, and between 1912 and 1916 Charles Jackson, beer retailer. We have to wait until 1916 for our first positive address, when Jas. W. Smith was identified as beer retailer, 365 Boldmere Road, placing it at the Erdington end, next door to the present *Cork & Bottle*, close to Sheffield Road.

John Greatrex, however, in the *Coldfield and Erdington and District Directory* of 1900, is shown on the corner of Boldmere Road and Highbridge Road as the occupier of the *Boldmere Tavern*. In 1901 it was renamed the *Station Inn*, with Emily Adams as tenant. She was followed by a succession of landlords until 1959, when it was demolished and the Boldmere Branch Library built on its site in 1960.

Station Inn, Boldmere Road, demolished in 1959.

Cook's Farm

Antrobus Road leads from Chester Road up the steep incline alongside the *New Oscott Tavern*, over the *Gibbet Hill* and down towards Boldmere Road, terminating opposite Highbridge Road.

When it was cut in the early 1900s the *New Oscott Tavern* had not been built, its site then being occupied by *Cook's Farm* and the single storey farmhouse, with its small duck pond near the front door, was where students from *New Oscott College* used to obtain dairy products. Adjacent to *Cook's Farm* was the *Brewery* owned by Mr Middleton.

Fernwood Grange

Long before Antrobus Road was cut, the man after whom the road was named came to live on a site overlooking Boldmere. Alfred Antrobus, a retired Birmingham jeweller in 1872 acquired an 8½ acre site at New Oscott, where he built himself a new house which he named *Fernwood*, and where he was to spend his retirement.

Fernwood Grange as it appeared in the 1920s.

He was able to devote himself to his passion for botany and the culture of trees and shrubs. During his years at *Fernwood*, he introduced, amongst other things, a variety of rare plants including some sub-tropical plants, which created considerable interest amongst natural history societies, many of whose members travelled from various parts of the country to visit the oasis of beauty which he had created.

On his death in 1907 he was buried in St Michael's Churchyard, Boldmere. *Fernwood* was then put up for sale. The auctioneer's catalogue stated:

> *"The garden upon which the late Mr Antrobus has, during the last 35 years, made lavish yet well considered outlays is unique. It contains perfect specimens of an endless variety of choice trees, shrubs and ferns and an enormous collection of rare herbaceous and other plants."*

Also on the site were stabling, a carriage-house, kennels, cow-house and piggeries.

The property was purchased by Edward Beston, a man of entirely different character. He was a wealthy bookmaker, who owned a large bookmaking business in Corporation Street, Birmingham.

Having purchased *Fernwood*, he enlarged the house, adding a music room, cinema, Abyssinian boudoir, Chinese lounge and a ballroom capable of holding 500 people. The new wing he added had twenty bedrooms, five bathrooms and a heated garage for four cars. Within the grounds were a switchback railway, peacocks and four St Bernard dogs, which he kept in large cages.

GOINGS ON AT FERNWOOD!

He entertained lavishly. Amongst his guests were many from the world of entertainment. Some elderly local people remember the "goings-on" at *Fernwood* and recall Daisy Dormer, a leading lady from one of the Birmingham shows, being installed at *Fernwood*, which caused a domestic crisis.

During the 1914-18 war he entertained wounded soldiers there and threw parties for them at Christmas time.

One of Beston's friends was Horatio Bottomley, a politician, race horse owner, founder of the magazine *John Bull* and a regular visitor to *Fernwood*. Their association was to end some years later when Beston had to flee the country, taking up residence for some time on the Continent.

RACING DISASTER LED TO EXILE

The one thing Beston and Bottomley had in common was horse racing. Bottomley was a betting man and had an idea to make a fortune by fixing a race. He chose Belgium for his scheme because of its less strict racing rules. He entered six of his horses in a race at the seaside town of Blankenburg and laid bets on each horse and the order in which they would finish. The jockeys, having been engaged by him, were instructed as to the order they were to finish. He and his associates in England laid heavy bets on the exact finishing order.

The horses were half-way round the course, which veered alongside the beach and sand dunes, when a heavy sea mist swept over the course so that the jockeys got hopelessly out of touch with each other. They crossed the finishing line in a hopeless jumble costing Bottomley and his English betting associates a fortune.

When Beston's exile finished he returned to England to live in Moseley. On his death he was buried in Witton Cemetery.

Attempts were made to sell *Fernwood Grange* without success, there being no takers. A decision was eventually taken to sell the fixtures and fittings after which the building was demolished.

The Lodge is all that remains of Fernwood Grange today.

Today the area covered by *Fernwood Grange* and its gardens is now a housing estate, the gardens of which are benefiting from trees and shrubs planted by Antrobus. The only structure remaining today, part of the *Grange*, is the lodge which stands on the corner of Chester Road and Fernwood Drive.

Schools from 1840

GREEN LANES SCHOOL

Education of the mind and enlightenment of the soul were designed to be combined, when in 1840 in nearby Green Lanes a Boy's School was erected. At week-ends the school was utilised, then each Sunday evening it was the venue for divine service. Apart from the Roman Catholic Chapel of St Nicholas, also built in 1840, which incorporated a school-room situated in Boldmere Road, there was no other Church of any denomination in the adjacent district of the *Coldfield*.

Girls and Infants School, Boldmere, built 1848.

BOLDMERE INFANTS SCHOOL

It was a further eight years before the next permanent educational establishment was built, this being the Girls' and Infants' School erected in 1848 on a plot of land fronting Boldmere Road. It was there shortly afterwards that morning service was held; W. K. Riland Bedford being the driving force for its existence.

Until the new school was erected the few people living on the *Coldfield* sent their children to the Town School. A record in *Town School's Log Book* for 1826 to 1904 shows that James Norris, the son of Joshua a sawmaker and his wife Lydia, of the *Coldfield*, was admitted to Town School on November 5th 1827. Their second son, Edward, was admitted on October 5th 1829. Also living on the *Coldfield* were Catherine Jones and her husband, Samuel, a wiredrawer at *Penns Mill*. They sent their son, William, to Town School on July 7th 1835. In 1848, the Reverend J. S. Moore is shown living in the School House.

When the Girls' and Infants' School was erected it stood in solitary isolation, being completely surrounded by fields, there being no other building in the immediate vicinity, and pupils would need to trek across the fields or down the narrow, unlit, hedged, lane later to be named Boldmere Road, along which carts would travel to and from *Spade Mill* on *Powell's Pool*.

USE OF BOLDMERE SCHOOLS FOR WORSHIP

The use of Green Lanes and the Girls' and Infants' School, Boldmere for worship by the local community was a temporary accommodation until a permanent church could be built, but it would be another nine years for this to be accomplished when St Michael's Church, in the Parish of Boldmere, was built without a spire.

On an 1857 map the Girls' and Infants' School was described as *National School* and by 1880 as *Corporation School* and on an 1882 map as *School*. However, now that the ecclesistical district of Boldmere was in being, the school soon acquired the title of Boldmere Girls' and Infants' School.

Heating for the school rooms was by coal fire and from the *Education Minutes* we learn that a fender was provided for the fire in March 1849, the cost of which was met by the Corporation.

It appears, however, that all was not well with the construction of the chimney and may have been creating consternation to the teacher and a delightful diversion for the pupils by smoke blowing back down the chimney when the wind was in the wrong direction. Consequently, the authorities in February 1850 directed that a mason be employed to "look at the chimney of the Coldfield School to see what can be done to make it draw better".

It was a local builder, Samuel Edwards, who was called in to alleviate the problem for which on 1st April 1850 his bill for £1.17s.0d (£1.85) for "chimney pipe etc., at the Infant School on the Coldfield" was met by the authorities.

Perhaps the smoke from the faulty chimney had affected the school decorations, for on September 2nd 1850 it was decided that the "rooms in the residence at the Coldfield School be coloured or papered."

About this time an addition was made to the school which needed drying out to make it useable by the children, so the mistress consumed extra coal on the fire in order to air the new part of her school, and for this was allowed, in January 1851, an extra ten shillings for the coals consumed.

PROBLEMS WITH THE PRIVY

Just three years after the school was built, problems regarding sanitation were experienced requiring Sutton's Education Committee, comprising the Reverend W. K. Riland Bedford, the Reverend W. G. Green, the Reverend S. C. Saxton and the Reverend J. Packwood, to discuss the problem affecting the Coldfield School, and after due deliberation on February 3rd 1851 to recommend that:

> "The present school privy at the Coldfield School be altered into a coal house and that a privy with a pig-sty be erected at a proper distance from the School".

Prior to the alterations to the privy the cesspool was to be opened up and examined, after which the coal house and pig-sty could be built according to the plan produced by Mr Cooper, the Bailiff, with a Mr Hill carrying out the work, which was to begin on Easter Monday, 1851. It is presumed the privy and pig-sty were built at a proper distance from the school and that due allowance was made for prevailing winds.

An indication that the school rooms would soon cease to be used for church services occured in September 1856 when, following divine service in the school room, the foundation stone of the new church on the hill was laid by the Right Honourable Helen, Countess of Bradford.

It is not until 1866 we learn the name of a teacher at the school. This is revealed in a directory of that date when Miss Maria Vaughton is identified as mistress of Boldmere Infants' School.

In a small community people provided their own entertainment. Boldmere School was an ideal venue for a series of entertainments in March 1884, evidenced by two surviving programmes listing a varied bill including a pianoforte duet, comic song, a reading, violin solo and a character song, all performed by local people. Admission was threepence and one penny.

On Monday, March 31st, 1884 a "Special Entertainment" was organised with the main attraction being Walter Rowton Esq., of London, who was booked to perform his "popular, humorous entertainments (which are most amusing and laughter provoking)" for which the public would pay one shilling for front seats and threepence for back seats. Tickets were available from Boldmere Provision Dealer, Mr Mansell.

Private Schools

In spite of the existence of the Girls' and Infants' School in Boldmere, a private school for young ladies flourished in the district for over thirty years. It was set up by two enterprising young ladies, who are named in *Kelly's Directory of Warwickshire*, 1890, as Misses Emmeline and Gertrude Hoare. Their young ladies school was established in Boldmere Road and was in existence between the years 1890 and 1924, which would indicate that they ran a highly successful establishment, satisfying an obvious need for such a considerable time.

It would also appear that the arts were not neglected for *Kelly's Directory of Warwickshire* of 1896 lists Mrs Lillian Stell of Boldmere Road, Professor of Music, and in those days houses of the middle class contained a piano. No doubt some of their children would be enrolled in Mrs Stell's music class.

Extension of Boldmere School

At the beginning of the new century, Mrs C. C. Holdcroft was listed as school mistress of Boldmere Schools, which by now had the parish rooms on one side and two almshouses on the other. In 1901 a new Infants' School was built up the hill next to the almshouses. This would house infants aged 5 to 7 years, whilst the Girls' School took girls aged 7 to 14 years. The old 1848 Girls' and

Boldmere Infants School, Boldmere Road, Built 1901 — demolished 1990.

Infants' School was to outlive this new school, which lasted until 1990 when it was demolished after ending its days as the Boldmere School Library.

Inside the new Infants' School, large windows provided light during the daytime, whilst long flexes with electric light bulbs hung from the very high pointed ceiling. A fireplace in the corner heated the room during Winter. The wooden desks each accommodated two children who had a box in which to hold their pens, pencils, crayons and books. Around the room tall wooden cupboards held stationery, books and other materials. Framed pictures hung from the walls and the children's artwork was conveniently pinned to the cupboard doors, also around the classroom walls.

A large doll's house stood in front of the class with its back to the wall and "Miss" surveyed the class from her desk near the corner of the classroom, comfortably siutated near the fire. Visitors to the school would have been surprised to find upon entering the classroom a maypole about eighteen feet tall within nine feet of the door.

Miss Doreen Ogden, a pupil at the school during the 1920s recalled the classroom had two classes in it; the right side was the top class and the left side was the second class. The babies' class was in a separate classroom.

She said the maypole was never taken outside. Each Friday the desks were pushed back to allow dancing around the maypole to take place.

There was also a see-saw and children had to sit very straight, with arms folded, and wait to be chosen, and put out at the front of the classroom.

Boldmere School, circa 1922, teacher Miss Randall. Mary Groves in centre of photograph (second row) still lives in the area.

HAVING YOUR OWN MAYPOLE WAS AN ADVANTAGE

Having its own maypole it appears, gave the Boldmere Girls an advantage over other schools, for during celebrations of the Coronation of King George V in June 1911 they took first prize in the maypole dancing competition.

During the 1914-18 War, Boldmere children were active in assisting the war effort and on one occasion undertook a very successful concert in Boldmere Parish Hall, part of the proceeds providing extra Christmas fare for wounded soldiers billeted in Sutton Park.

THE 1928 PAGEANT

In 1928 a pageant was planned to celebrate the 400th Anniversary of Sutton Coldfield's Royal Charter, which had been presented by Henry VIII to Sutton in 1528. Local schools, including Boldmere, were visited to select children with flaxen hair and blue eyes to act as Anglo Saxons in the pageant, which was to be held in Sutton Park. Miss Ogden said she didn't meet the specifications so wasn't chosen.

Accommodation at the school in 1928 was recorded as 214 for the girls, with an average attendance of 91%, and 144 for the infants, with the average attendance being 79%.

Once a week during the Summer in the 1930s a party of girls would be taken to *Keepers Pool* in Sutton Park for swimming. Misses Miller and Jones would take the group, consisting of swimmers and a few non-swimmers, and give them a swimming lesson at the baths.

The Modern Boldmere School

The original Infants' and Girls' School, erected in 1848, served the children of the district for about ninety years, but it was felt in the 1930s that with the growth of the district, larger and more modern premises were needed, and so by 1938 two large school blocks, consisting of four new schools for Senior Boys, Senior Girls, Junior Mixed and Infants had been erected at a cost of approximately £70,000 and were officially opened by Kenneth Lindsay, Parliamentary Secretary to the Board of Education. Headmaster of the Senior Boys' School was Mr F. Chapman and Miss A. C. Barton was Headmistress of the Senior Girls' School.

With the outbreak of the Second World War in September 1939 the old Girls' and Infants' School was put to use as an ambulance station with many local ladies engaged in driving ambulances and carrying out other necessary war duties there.

St Michaels Church Hall and Girls and Infants School, Boldmere Road

After the War it was used for various activites, including accommodation for evening classes for art, until the present time when it is now used as a clinic.

Boldmere Senior Boys' and Senior Girls' Schools, later to become Boldmere High School, survived until the 1970s, when during education re-organisation they were closed, although the Infants' and Junior Schools, in Cofield Road are still in use.

Boldmere Infants School, Cofield Road, Boldmere (built 1938).

Sport in Boldmere

Perhaps the first sporting activities in the Coldfield may be attributed to swimming and fishing in *Powell's Pool*, also rabbiting and archery on the heathland. In fact the Reverend E. H. Kittoe M.A., Vicar of St Michael's Church, Boldmere 1857 - 1894 was fully aware of local rabbiting for often his sermons would be interrupted by the sound of gunfire and he would announce to his congregation "there goes another of my rabbits".

Swimming — Boldmere Swimming Club

Boldmere Swimming Club was formed in the nineteenth century as the district was growing, and one of their programmes dated 1903 still exists advertising the seventh annual water carnival to be held on August 15th, 1903 at *Powell's Pool*. Their first water carnival was held at *Powell's* in 1886, but swimming activities by individuals and clubs must have been taking place at the pool since the time of its creation in 1730.

Until *Powell's Pool* was purchased by the Corporation, it had been owned by the Holt and the Somerville family and so had remained outside the park until its purchase by Sutton Corporation when it became part of the park.

In addition to *Powell's Pool*, Boldmere Swimming Club also took advantage of the baths at *Keeper's Pool* for we see in the *Park and Estates Committee 1891 Annual Report* that Boldmere Swimming Club had made their "usual application to use the baths", for which they paid the annual charge of £2.00.

By 1904, however, it was reported by the Park and Estates Committee that Boldmere Swimming Club had the use of *Powell's Pool* for their early morning swim.

COST PROBLEMS WITH POWELL'S POOL

Problems were encountered by the Club in 1907, which caused the members to change their venue, for at their Annual Meeting on 4th May, 1907 held at the *Sutton Park Hotel*, it was revealed that the terms offered by the Powell's Pool Company for continued use of the dressing sheds were considered prohibitive. Consequently, they moved to a pool offering more reasonable terms. To confirm they had made the correct decision to move, one of the members pointed out the balance sheet showed a surplus of £1.11s.6d, whereas staying at *Powell's* would have created a deficiency of between £10 - £12.

At the end of 1905 membership of the Club totalled nearly 400, but in 1906 membership fell to 336, which one member blamed on having to move.

The sad consequences of the 1914-18 War resulted in many young members of the Boldmere Swimming Club losing their lives. After the War a fitting memorial to them was placed near the dam of *Powell's Pool*. It consisted of two figures: a tutor and pupil with an inscription which read;

> *"Erected by the Boldmere Swimming Club and friends to the memory of members of the Club who made the great sacrifice for their King and Country in the terrible War 1914-1918"*

The statue now stands outside Wyndley Swimming Baths.

Benjamin Creswick's little bronze statue in its present position outside Wyndley Swimming Baths.

Swimming at *Powell's Pool* is now discouraged. It was once the regular venue for Boldmere Swimming Club for many years. Each year they would hold their Annual General Meeting at the *Sutton Park Hotel*.

Sutton Sailing Club c.1956

In the 1920s the swimmers used the derelict water-mill as changing rooms. One local resident and member of the Club recalls that the mill had cold earth floors.

Children from local schools were encouraged to go swimming in the park, but always under the supervision of the teachers, and always at the swimming baths at *Keeper's Pool*.

The Sea Scouts training ship at Powells Pool.

FISHING

One of the oldest sports *Powell's Pool* caters for is fishing. Since the pool was created in 1730, until the present day, enthusiastic men and boys line the banks during the season. Unfortunately, they are no longer able to hire boats to fish from as they were all removed in 1955.

Sutton Sailing Club

Adjacent to the pool is Sutton Sailing Club with a membership exceeding 500. Whilst enjoying their sport, they also provide pleasant relaxing entertainment for the many visitors and picnickers attracted there.

The pool was de-silted in 1938, allowing the boats more freedom over a larger area and improvements to their headquarters were made, including a new hardstanding on which boats not in use could be stored.

The Club's many competitions throughout the year attract competitors from far afield.

Boldmere Municipal Golf Club

Boldmere Municipal Golf Course, designed in 1933 by Clive Bretherton as a nine-hole course, was opened in 1935 and extended to eighteen-holes after the 1939-45 War. Its entrance is in Monmouth Drive, close to the Clubhouse, where meals and refreshments are served. The course runs from Stonehouse Road to Banners Gate, returning alongside the park and *Powell's Pool*, a total distance of 4,506 yards.

The entrance to Boldmere Golf Club and Sutton Sailing Club in Monmouth Drive.

There have been only three club professionals. The first, Arthur Ricketts, was succeeded by Jim Bayliss. The present professional, Trevor Short, ably assisted by his wife Shirley, also runs a well-stocked golf shop on site where all the golfing equipment and clothing required may be obtained, all at big discounts.

In August 1992, the 40th Anniversary, the World's longest running Municipal Pro-Am Golf Tournament was held by Boldmere Golf Club. It was also the first time in this country that the PGA had run a municipal pro-am tournament.

The Arthur Price of England Perpetual Trophy was won by J. Rhodes of South Staffs Golf Club with a score of 58. Thirty teams, each consisting of a professional and three amateurs, competed for the *Stan Jackson Pro-Am Cup*, with professional Gerry Haines taking the Cup and his three amateur team mates from Boldmere Golf Club, John Turner, Warren Glen and David Clark, each receiving a rose bowl.

Boldmere St Michael's Football Club

A name that has figured prominently in amateur football, in Sutton Coldfield, for over 110 years is Boldmere St Michael's Football Club, whose ground in Church Road is just below St Michael's Church, the spire of which can be seen rising majestically above a screen of trees.

The Club was founded in 1883 from a bible class of St Michael's Church. Its playing strength was reduced during the 1914-1918 War, when many players had to report for active service. In 1922 it survived a further setback when the senior players left to form another club, which has since ceased to exist.

During the 1920s the team was in dispute with the Church when it wanted to charge an entrance fee to the ground, and for a while the club moved to another ground owned by Anstey College, but moved back to Church Road when the dispute was settled.

In the 1930s the official link with the Church was broken although there still remains a close unofficial connection.

1938 BROUGHT A NEW PAVILION

They entered the Central Amateur League in 1938, but football activity was soon to be interupted by the outbreak of the 1939-1945 War. Also, in 1938, Sutton Corporation who had purchased the ground for £2500, were anxious to help the Club and assisted financially towards the cost of a new football pavilion.

During the War the ground was requisitioned by the Home Office for use by the Auxilliary Fire Service. Although the Fire Service took possession of the pavilion in 1940 the football club managed to use the field.

OTHER CLUBS USED THE FIELD

Over the years, Boldmere St Michael's Football Club, was not the only club to make use of the field. In 1900, the *Park and Estates Committee Annual Report* states that the ground at Boldmere was rented by the L & NWR employees' Football Club during the Winter months, previously they had played in Sutton Park, and during the Summer it was occupied by Boldmere Cricket Club and then in 1901 by Sutton Park Cricket Club.

No cricket was played at the Church Road ground during the War, but by 1945, whilst the AFS still occupied the pavilion, Boldmere St Michael's Football Club was again using the pitch.

In 1946 the ground was de-requisitioned and negotiations commenced with the Home Office for the amount of compensation to be paid for damage to the ground and buildings. That year the ground was let to Boldmere St Michael's Football Club.

Renovations to the pavilion were completed by 1947 and the Club took over a seasonal tenancy at a rental of £56 p.a. The huts erected by the AFS were removed, and negotiations were entered into with the Home Office for the acquisition of the brick control room and garage.

Two years later in 1949 a seven year lease was offered to the Club at a rental of £75 p.a., and the Club was given permission to terrace part of the ground. During the 1920s the pitch ran from the top to the bottom of the field, but this was later altered so that the pitch now runs along the field.

During the 1947-1948, season they reached the Amateur Football Final, playing at Villa Park in front of a 10,000 crowd. They drew with Cambridge 1:1.

Since the 1940s, when they had a strong team which played in the Birmingham and District League, a semi-professional league, they have had mixed fortunes, but their ambitions remain high, for it is their future aim to join the Southern League.

Harold Spencer, a stalwart of the Club and now in his eighties, played for the Club from the 1920s until the late 1950s when he would occasionally turn out even though he was in his fifties.

SEVERAL BOLDMERE PLAYERS BECAME PROFESSIONALS

One Boldmere player who made his mark professionally was Harry Parkes, whose talents were recognised by Aston Villa, who snapped him up. Many other Boldmere players over the years were also signed up by professional football league clubs including P. Richardson, K. Norman and A. Pollard to Aston Villa: D. Moss to Cardiff City: W. Soden to Coventry City: J. Lane to Birmingham City and H. Wright to West Bromwich Albion.

In 1971 a disastrous fire destroyed the 1938 wooden pavilion along with equipment and many precious records. The Club set to and soon erected a more substantial and larger pavilion in brick on the site of the old building.

By March 1990 a new venture was accomplished when, through a sponsorship deal with Mitchells & Butlers, they erected floodlights at the ground. These were used officially in March for the match against Stapenhill.

Map of Boldmere c.1906

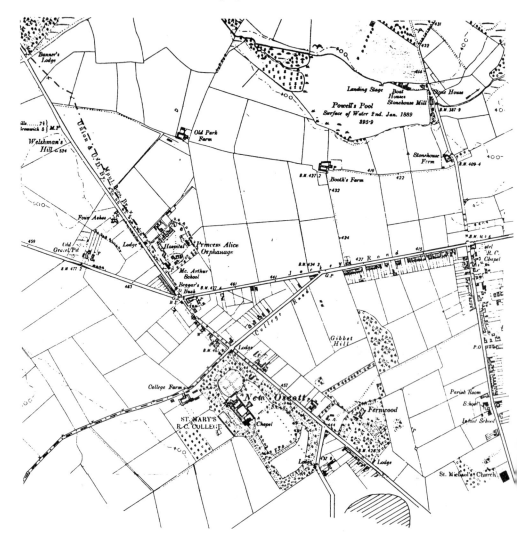

Part of Ordnance Survey 6" : 1 mile, second edition 1904 with approximate site of Baldmoor Lake shown at the bottom cross hatched.

PART 2

The Growth of Boldmere to 1900

The pace of building in the Coldfield slowly gathered momentum. The 1841 census lists people living in the district, some of whom were connected with the watermill at *Powell's Pool*, including John Willets, aged 25, forgeman; John Page, 35 years old, spade maker; John Harris, 50 and Henry Astbury, 30, sawmaker and spade maker respectively. Francis Parkes, who ran the mill built his house *Stonehouse* on the bank of the pool in 1844. J. H. Parkes, a future Sutton Mayor was born there in 1850.

William Yates aged 75 is shown as a farmer, but the name of his farm is not stated. His wife Ann was 60 years old, and they employed 12 year old George Bowden as a servant. Jane Starkey was "schoolmistress" but the name of her school not identified.

A number of people were shown to be living at Baldmoor Lake, the name of which was to be of significance to the district.

St. Michael's Church

The erection of a girls' and infants school in 1848 and the Church of St Michael in 1857, was an indication of the increase in local population, although the Church was built in rural surroundings only sparsely populated; there were a few wealthy people locally, including businessmen, and owners of factories in Birmingham; and a smattering of artisans, farmers, public servants, shopkeepers, labourers and servants.

THE BIRMINGHAM TO SUTTON RAILWAY

It was the opening of the Birmingham to Sutton Railway line in 1862, and later the electric tramway, which gave impetus to the growth in population in the new district of Boldmere. Starting at the Erdington end, new houses with long front gardens gradually make their way up the hill to the Church, then down towards Jockey Road where a mixture of shops and houses was erected: Boldmere Road being then still a narrow tree-lined thoroughfare.

Prior to this, the main area of development from the 1840s until 1857 was from the *Sutton Park Inn* to where Highbridge Road would eventually be cut. The 1857 map whilst showing existing roads does not name them, but we know them as Boldmere Road, Stonehouse Road, Jockey Lane, Sheffield Road, and Gate Lane, but Church Road was the only one indicated.

The Church of St Michaels, Boldmere. Consecrated 1857. It was enlarged in 1871.

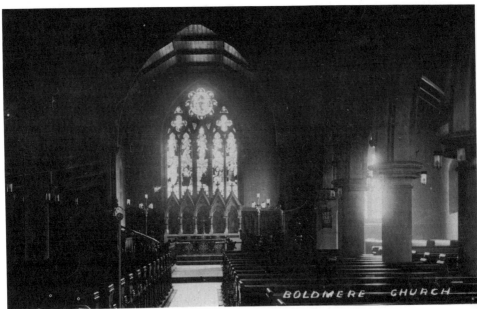

Postcard dated 1908, showing interior of the Church of St Michael, Boldmere.

On 4th March 1858, the ecclesiastical parish of Boldmere was formed. The Reverend W. K. Riland Bedford in 1891 made an observation on the growth of Boldmere when he wrote:

> "Up to the date of the railway (1862) communication with Birmingham was carried on by means of omnibuses drawn by two, three or four horses, which took the average time of eighty minutes for the journey from Sutton to Birmingham.
>
> It was natural during the existence of this mode of intercommunication that part of the Parish which lay nearest to Birmingham Road should develop most rapidly, and this led first to the formation of an ecclesistical district and then to the foundation of a Church and Parish to which the name Boldmere was given from the situation of the Church on the eminence above Baldmoor Lake upon Chester Road".

During the 1860s, land in the Boldmere district was sold for building purposes and continued through to the 1930s when most of the available land was developed.

FROM COLDFIELD TO BOLDMERE

In 1861 the name of the district was still without its final form, as the *Borough of Sutton Coldfield Rate Book* of 1861 describes the Reverend W. K. Riland Bedford, as owner of plantations in the *Coldfield* or *Bolemere*, and Thomas Cornforth, as occupying land at *Bolemere Lake*. By 1864, however, the *Post Office Directory of Warwickshire* is quite specific when it refers to two almshouses to be erected at Boldmere, with Frederick Allen, The Firs, Boldmere; Thomas Instone, Boldmere House, and William Harrison, farmer, Boldmere. So the name was now firmly established.

By 1880 Church Road was cut and continued over the other side of Boldmere Road. Station Road was now in existence, with Western Road connecting with Highbridge Road. The future Antrobus Road was indicated but still to be made.

THE SPIRE ADDED TO ST MICHAEL'S CHURCH

In 1871 the spire and north aisle of St Michael's Church, Boldmere were built at a cost of £1,400. A few years later in 1877 *The Birches*, Jockey Road was built. This was to become the new headquarters of Sutton Coldfield Conservative Club, which was founded in April 1913.

Two almshouses next to the Girls' and Infants' School in Boldmere Road were erected in 1864. Across the other side of the road, on the corner of Boldmere and Station Roads, a large house called *Normanhurst* was erected. This survived until the mid 1900s when, during redevelopment, it was demolished and a number of new properties built in its extensive grounds.

The map of 1882 shows that Park Lane had not yet been changed to Stonehouse Road and that the old water-mill at *Powell's Pool* was described as "steel rolling". Up at the *Beggars Bush*, the second *Bush Inn* was firmly established and the original *Bush Inn* now converted to three cottages.

Almshouses, Boldmere Road. Built circa 1865.

Both the above certificate and the one on the opposite page belong to Hilda Jeffs:, a relative of Mrs Irene Ducker.

RULES

1. Morning School to be held at The Boldmere School, from 9-45 to 10-45.
   Afternoon School to be held at The Boldmere School, from 2-45 to 3-45.

2. Scholars not to be enrolled on the School Register until they have attended regularly for one month, when a card of membership will be given, and the same must be brought at the close of the year, to be filled in and signed by the Vicar or Hon. Secretary. A scholar failing to do this will not be admitted to the Treat.

3. The maximum number of marks to be eight; two for attendance, three for lessons, and three for conduct..

4. Scholars not arriving before prayers to forfeit one attendance mark.

5. The marks to be entered by the Teachers in the Class Registers, which must be given every three months to the Vicar or Hon. Secretary for examination and entry into the School Register.

6. The promotion of Scholars and the adjustment of the Classes to take place at the beginning of each year, when Prizes will be given to the deserving Scholars in each Class for the previous year.

7. Scholars not to be admitted to the Treat unless they have made half the Marks attainable.

The Rules above are a reproduction of those appearing on the reverse of the certificate illustrated alongside.

A. E. R. BEDFORD. *Vicar*

.... *Hon. Secretary*

St. Michael's Church, Boldmere.
SUNDAY SCHOOL.

CARD ✛ OF ✛ MEMBERSHIP,

Presented to *Hilda Jeffs*
Jul. 1896.
A. E. R. Bedford Vicar.

Marks Attainable.		Marks Gained.		During the year.	SIGNED BY
Morning.	Afternoon.	Morning.	Afternoon.		
	360		5	1896	A. E. R. Bedford.
416	416	69	334	1897	A. E. R. Bedford.
416	408	39	280	1898	A. E. R. B.
416	408	–	353	1899	A. E. R. B.
408	408	–	200	1900	A. E. R. B.
416	416	..	375	1901	J. S.
416	416	–	372	1902	A. E. R. B.
416	416	–	367	1903	J. A. Holroyd
416	416	–	388	1904	A. E. R. B.
424	424	–	389	1905	H. Hamburg Baker
416	416	309	388	1906	Allen Jones
	416		228	1907	For the Rule see p.

HIGHBRIDGE ROAD CONCERN

In 1890 Boldmere was referred to in a *Health and Highways Report* as "the black spot of the Borough", and in particular the condition of Highbridge Road was causing concern to those who used it, being a quagmire in Winter and saturated in organic filth. The Committee excused themselves from improving it in consequence of it being private property.

Alderman Walters said he denied the Committee wished to neglect Boldmere and it was fortunate that, with the exception of about 200 yards, the whole of the roads in Boldmere would be main roads, repairable by the County from the beginning of 1891.

POPULATION REACHED 1490 BY 1859

At the end of 1859 the area of Boldmere covered 1,051 acres and had a population of 1,490. In 1898 building continued in Highbridge Road and *Tintern Villas* were erected.

A poll of the Burgesses resulted in the defeat of a scheme to purchase the gas undertaking in the town, but the voters of Wylde Green, Boldmere and Chester Road expressed an interest in obtaining a gas supply from Birmingham.

Building land in Boldmere was still being sold; in 1896 a sale of land bounded by Sheffield Road, Boldmere Road and Chester Road, enabled Sheffield Road to be widened.

Grove Cottage

Just inside Highbridge Road, behind the present Branch Library, and hidden by a tall hedge, is *Grove Cottage*. The earliest recorded date for this building is 1850. The owner at that time was John Smith. By 1861, 48 years old John James, agricultural labourer, is owner occupier. Living with him was his wife, 48 year old Mary, and daughter Celia. aged 22. She was a dressmaker. From then until the present day there has been a regular turnover of owners and occupiers, as fully described by Mrs Betty May in her article, *The Adventures of a Novice in the Local History Wonderland*, published in *Vol 2: Proceedings of the Sutton Coldfield Local History Group.*

Grove Cottage, Highbridge Road, Boldmere.

Tintern Villas, Highbridge Road, Boldmere. Built 1898.

Highbridge Road in 1937.

Building continued apace, and in 1900, next to *Tintern Villas* a further four houses were erected, whilst across the road in Boldmere Road the new Boldmere Infants' School was built in 1901 adjacent to the almshouses. The School's last days were occupied as the library to the more modern school erected in the 1930s in Cofield Road.

Little Boldmere

At the start of the new century some local Boldmere traders who carried adverts in the *Sutton and Erdington District Directory* were:

> *W. Lyons, cash grocers, Boldmere Road,* Ye Old Gayte Inn, *proprietor David Capewell, Boldmere Road, George Davis & Son, builders, Boldmere Road, and Jennings Boot Depot, Boldmere Road.*

THE BIRD BAKERY

The Erdington end of Boldmere Road joins Chester Road close to where Sheffield Road meets Boldmere Road. There can be found a cluster of shops each occupied by a small trader. These shops were erected at the turn of the century between 1899 and 1903. One business which survived for over 70 years

Little Boldmere circa 1908.

until 1968 was that of Edwin J. Bird & Son, bakers, at No 384. The business was actually started by the grandmother of Mr Brian John Bird when she married Edwin Bird and moved from her Erdington business into the first premises in Sheffield Road and set up as a baker with her new husband, who quickly became established in the bakery trade.

In 1903 they had new premises erected in Boldmere Road to their own specification by Squires the Builders, where they built up a thriving business. Their son, Walter James Bird, joined his father when he was able and subsequently grandson, Brian John Bird, joined his father Walter, who had eventually succeeded the business. Walter died in 1964 and four years later Brian closed down, and so a long established Boldmere bakery business came to an end.

The Bird bakery premises are now occupied by Astbury Kilby & Co Ltd, Electrical Engineering Distributors and the original ovens are still in existence.

This photograph taken in 1905 shows Boldmere Road, Wylde Green, lined with trees and the local shops. Third from the left is a butchers with huge portions of meat hung up outside. Unfortunately the price of the meat has risen just as much as Boldmere Road has changed over recent years.

A 1905 photograph looking at the shops at the Erdington end of Boldmere Road from Chester Road sees six mature trees lining the pavement. Today this section of the pavement has been cut away to provide parking space for motor vehicles and the trees have gone.

A LEGACY OF THE SPADE MILL

The many ash trees about the Boldmere district were planted by the Parkes family, owners of *Spade Mill* situated at *Powell's Pool*. It was intended that when they reached maturity they would be used to provide handles for the thousands of spades and forks produced at the Mill, but apparently they were not required as sufficient quantities of wood for the purpose were imported from abroad. So the ash trees were to remain to grace the district as a legacy of the Parkes family and *Spade Mill*.

In the 1905 photograph the nearest shop is *Eastman's Butchers,* and just three shops up the road is another butcher's shop with huge portions of meat hung up outside. Unfortunately none of the Boldmere properties were given numbers until about the 1920s. People identified the buildings by the name plaques affixed to the walls, which must have made it very difficult for the postman who had to memorise either the names of all the residents and where they lived, or memorise the names of the properties identifiable by the plaques.

Trying to trace where people were located through the listing in the various directories was partly possible if they were listed one property after another, that is until they started listing people in alphabetical order: then it became impossible to trace where they lived.

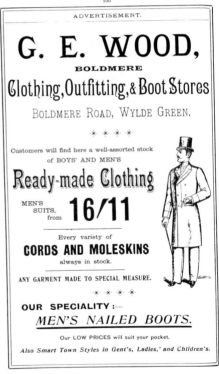

Advertisements from the Sutton Coldfield Directory of 1901-2.

ROAD WIDENED

At the time Boldmere Road was quite narrow with a row of shops at each end. The Erdington end of Boldmere Road was referred to by the locals as *Little Boldmere*. Trees lined the pavements which made the road look even narrower than it was. The trees ran the whole length of Boldmere Road.

As traffic along Boldmere Road increased over the years it was found necessary to reduce the width of the pavements in front of the shops to allow cars to park and to enable the traffic to flow more freely. This also had the effect of reducing the numbers of trees on the pavements and opening up the area so that the buildings on either side of the road could now be seen.

Shops in Boldmere Road opposite Sheffield Road.

Bus Services Introduced

The Midland Red in 1913 put on a single decker bus service from Birmingham to Sutton which passed down Jockey Road and through Boldmere. Later Boldmere was provided with its own bus service by Midland Red, which started from The Parade, Sutton and ran down Jockey Road and along Boldmere Road.

These single deckers had their destination board running along the sides of the bus, just below the windows. They had solid tyres, a bulbous horn with which the driver could warn unwary pedestrians, and a single main headlamp suspended from the leading edge of the roof, just above the driver's head, at the front of the bus.

And you moan about today's buses! How would you like this rolling up at the bus stop one wet and windy day? This bus was one of the Midland Red's Sutton Fleet. It ran between Boldmere Road, Jockey Road and Sutton Parade. Here it is pictured with its driver and a "clippie".

The driver wore a white coat and a flat hat and he was assisted by a "clippie" to collect the fares. She carried a pack of tickets and a small machine suspended by a leather strap from her shoulders to her waist. With this machine she would clip a hole in the ticket to indicate where the passenger boarded the bus. She wore a dark uniform consisting of jacket and skirt and she also wore a hat.

Boldmere Road in 1908.

Chester Road Baptist Church

Having started with a few people meeting in a home and later moving to Green Lanes School (now Wylde Green Junior and Infants School) to hold services, Chester Road Baptist Church was formed on October 16th 1905. By that time the members were worshipping in a temporary building (still in use!) on the Boldmere Road and the Sunday School met in Boldmere Road Post Office.

Its present building, sited strategically on the corner of Boldmere Road and Chester Road was opened in 1913 and additional rooms have been added over the years.

The first minister was the Rev. G. W. Bevan and since then the church has had eight ministers. From the church three men entered the ministry and six people went overseas as missionaries.

Today the church is active in serving the community in many different ways, notably amongst children and young people through the Junior Church and Boys' and Girls' Brigades and encouraging those with learning difficulties by being responsible for a group home and running weekly clubs.

Wylde Green United Reformed Church

The United Reformed Church which is situated at the junction of Britwell Road and Highbridge Road, has been in existence since 1900, when it was known as Wylde Green Congregational Church. The name changed in 1972

Wylde Green United Reformed Church, Britwell Road.

as the result of a national union of Congregational churches and The Presbyterian Church of England.

The present church building was erected in 1904, and the main hall — The Britwell Hall — in 1933. In 1975, a set of modern rooms were built on the site of the original "tin tabernacle".

During its life, the church has had eleven ministers, and at present has 180 members. It is particularly involved in work amongst children and young people, although a wide range of activities for all ages take place on its premises. It also has a notable choir, which has in recent years won competitions in music festivals at Lichfield and Derby, and has sung in many cathedrals, including Lichfield and Birmingham.

Boldmere Methodist Church

Boldmere Methodist Church originated as the Boldmere Brotherhood, which began in 1911 when a group of friends would hold their meetings at *Powell's Pool*.

A site for their Church was found in Boldmere Road, the builder being G. T. Stephens, and the stone laying ceremony took place in May 1912. An extension was added after the First World War. They bought an army hut which had been left in Sutton Park since 1918 and this later became the Boldmere Branch Library.

After the Second World War, with the congregation greatly decreased, it was suggested the Brotherhood joined the Methodist Church. In 1948 the Boldmere Hall was made available to the Sutton Methodist Circuit for the purpose of conducting social and religious activities, and later the whole building was handed over.

Methodist Church, Boldmere Road.

In 1948 membership was just sixteen, by 1972 the membership had increased to 115. When in 1960 the New Branch Library was built, the Methodist Church bought back its army hut.

In 1972 the Church was completely rebuilt and refurbished inside, the familiar exterior of the building remained unchanged.

The Spinney

One piece of land situated in the middle of the *Coldfield* near the top of Gibbett Hill that was to remain free of development from the time of the 1824 enclosures until the present day is known by local people as the Spinney, although such a name does not appear on any map. Originally it was about five acres in extent, but over the passage of time it has been reduced to just over three acres, and since 1857 when the shape of the spinney first appeared as such on any map, but without an official name, it has remained a pocket of woodland consisting of oaks and undergrowth.

Until new roads were laid out near the spinney in the 1930s access was by means of a path running next to *Middleton's Brewery* on the Chester Road and up the hill. Development of the *Coldfield* was unhurried until the coming of

"The Spinney" from Antrobus Road entrance, November 1990.

the railway in 1862 when commuters by rail and tram from Birmingham discovered *Boldmere* to be a nice rural retreat and house building gathered pace.

By the 1930s most of the area had been developed and access to the spinney was obtained via three new roads: Antrobus Road, Oakwood Road and Maxstoke Road.

This pocket of woodland was at some time after the first World War acquired freehold by John White of Handsworth and a furniture manufacturer, Max Nepolsky, of Nottingham, who was also an ex Polish Army Officer. As a token of his gratitude for the shelter and hospitality this Country afforded him, he made a gift in 1930 of this small wooded area to the Corporation of Sutton Coldfield on condition:

> *"they would not do or cause to be done upon the land any act or thing deemed to be a nuisance, annoyance or disturbance to the owners or occupiers of the adjoining land, nor should they allow any structure or building other than shelters or public conveniences to be erected. Neither should they allow any buildings or dispensing machines where intoxicating drink may be manufactured, bought or sold".*

The Corporation was put to the test in 1984 as a result of mounds of soil from the Wyndley area being tipped some years before to prevent damage and destruction to the wooded area by footballers. However, in 1984 this had the effect of attracting hundreds of youths on their BMX bikes, which had been invented to traverse rough terrain, and they had found the mounds of earth ideal for this purpose.

This, however, had an adverse effect upon the comfort of the local residents because of the noise, bad language, fighting and all the other problems created by hordes of youths intent on enjoying themselves away from their own districts.

Local Councillors were at first unhelpful when approached to try to resolve the problem, saying the area was designated a public open space and there was nothing they could do to stop the nuisance. That was until the Conditions of the Deed of Gift were drawn to their attention, and then measures were eventually taken to stamp out the hordes descending on what was a quiet suburban district, much to the relief of the local residents.

Encouragement was given to the area when the Urban Wildlife Trust took an interest and some planting was done which helped to repair some of the damage.

Today the spinney is once again a tranquil place where people can enjoy its beauty and take a quiet stroll.

EARLY COMMUTERS

In addition to the railway from Birmingham to Sutton enabling people to commute from Boldmere, passengers alighting from the tram at the Erdington Terminus would make their way to the Boldmere entrance to Sutton Park by walking down Boldmere Road. This would help stimulate trade for the shopkeepers and provide welcome custom for the various inns and public houses along the way.

Boldmere Road, leading to Sutton Park.

The *Sutton News* reported on October 4th, 1913 that Sutton Park Accounts showed an excess expenditure of £532.6s.0d., but most of this was accounted for by the erection of *Boldmere Lodge* at a cost of £425. It was considered necessary to build the lodge to deal with the increased numbers of visitors now using this entrance.

Boldmere Lodge, Sutton Park.

Local Politics

At a meeting of the Electors held at Boldmere Girls School in 1912 a Mr Marston remarked on the astonishing growth of Boldmere.

It was in 1913 that *The Birches*, a large house in Jockey Road, Boldmere, was leased out to the Sutton Coldfield Conservative Club, which had been founded on April 26th, 1913. *The Birches* was a substantial building with a large garden, which was ideal for holding garden parties and other events. It stands fronting Jockey Road and its appearance in 1913 bore no resemblance to that of today.

It had a hedge nearly five feet tall and most of the front of the house was covered in ivy. Now devoid of its ivy and hedge the building has been considerably renovated. A tall fence replaces the hedge, behind which plenty of parking space exists for members cars, and its extensive garden now contains a well kept bowling green.

After four years *The Birches*, which had been built in 1877 was bought by the Conservative Club for £2,500. At today's prices, together with its 2¼ acres of prime building land, it would be worth well over a quarter of a million pounds.

The Conservative Club House
"The Birches"

A Garden Party held
at "The Birches"
in June 1913.

The Club was originally a Bowls Club and the Green still remains.

At the Boldmere Burgess Association Meeting held at the Boldmere Parish Rooms on October 4th 1913 it was stated a petition had been presented to the Town Council signed by all the residents in the section of Boldmere Road from Highbridge Road to Station Road, protesting against the erection of telegraph poles. Apparently the Council intended to resist the Postmaster-General in this matter.

POOR COMMUNICATION WITH THE FIRE BRIGADE

Another tenant, who lived in Mayfield Road, pointed out that there were no means of communication with Sutton Fire Station. He said there was no call office within half a mile, and in case of fire the caller would have to go to either Wylde Green Post Office or to Boldmere Road; by which time they would be burnt out. He suggested a call box be installed in the neighbourhood of Jockey Road.

On October 10th, 1914 at the Boldmere Burgess Association Meeting, held at the *Boldmere Parish Rooms*, reference was made to a request made at the 1913 meeting to install a fire alarm box in Jockey Road. Since then application had been made to the Chairman of the Fire Brigade Committee and they were pleased to notice the request had been carried out.

Reference was also made to a fire in Boldmere Road in May 1912, following which there had been much correspondence in the *Sutton News* and the general feeling was that the Fire Brigade was not equal to any emergency. In the Council Chamber one of the representatives of the Ward said that apparatus in the alarm box was nothing but rubbish.

Mr Spittle said a fire had occurred near to his own house in May 1914 and he was very well pleased with the turnout on that occasion. He said "they seemed to know what to do" and he was inclined to think that since the 1912 fire the Brigade had been put on a satisfactory footing, to which the meeting agreed. Also, a permanent man had been put in charge and a fire box had been placed in Jockey Road. He maintained, however, it was essential they should have a motor fire engine.

INADEQUATE STREET LIGHTING

The question of lighting at the corner of Boldmere Road, Chester Road and Gravelly Lane was raised. It was considered insufficient for such a dangerous corner. Apparently, attached to a central post were four incandescent lights, three of which had broken mantles.

The lights could not be seen when approaching from Sheffield Road or from the direction of Oscott. It was suggested a light on each corner would be preferable. But, if it was necessary to have a light in the centre because of the ventilating shaft, it would be more effective if moved a yard or more from the present position.

Criticism was also made of the poor lighting in Jockey Road between Somerville Road and Mayfield Road. These matters were to be brought to the attention of the Borough Surveyor. In June 1914 the Electricity Committee reported that the mains extension for Boldmere Road was almost complete, and in the same year Boldmere Church was connected to the mains.

Boldmere and the 1914-18 War

The year 1914 was the year that the Great War, that was to claim many lives, broke out in Europe. Nearer home, for the duration of the War, a Civil Defence Camp was built near *Powell's Pool* and many Boldmere families provided billets

Troops during training in Sutton Park

to hundreds of young men serving in the Royal Warwickshire Regiment, who did their military training in Sutton Park before being sent to the Front in Europe.

The people of Boldmere organised many fund raising events, for the War Effort, to provide comforts for the soldiers, including the many wounded soldiers who came to Sutton Park to recuperate.

Peace was declared in 1918 and people were able to settle down to a more normal way of life and indulge in sporting and cultural activities.

Highbury Theatre Group

One group of young people in 1924 started meeting in a house called *Highbury* rehearsing plays. They struggled on using different private houses and halls which were hired to put on their plays. In 1937, after many unsuccessful attempts, they secured a plot of land in Sheffield Road, and with only £40 in the kitty, set about building their own theatre, which they named *The Highbury*.

The work of planning and construction etc. was all carried out by voluntary labour. A considerable amount of the construction was done by two actresses.

The Second World War did not deter them. Much carpeting and many seats were purchased when the *Prince of Wales Theatre*, Birmingham was demolished

Highbury Little Theatre, Sheffield Road.

during a air raid. The curtain finally went up for the first time on May 22nd 1942; the first play being Shaw's "Arms and the Man". The same play was put on again to celebrate the Theatre's Twenty First Birthday with John English, founder and first director, and three of the original cast.

In 1960 they purchased an adjoining plot of land and a building fund of £6,000 was launched. Since then building and extensions have been added so that over fifty years later those two young actresses, who had put in so much time and labour, would hardly recognise the theatre as it is today.

The Start of Traffic Problems

At the time of the founding of the Highbury Theatre Group in 1925 the flow of traffic along Boldmere Road was very sparse. In fact, Miss Ogden of Stonehouse Road, Boldmere who was a pupil at the Girls School in Boldmere Road in the 1920s, said of the traffic "when we were out at play if a car went down Boldmere Road we all ran to the fence to look at it and waved to it because it was so unusual".

It was about this time that Park Lane, which ran from Boldmere Gate to Jockey Road changed its name to Stonehouse Road.

The borough of Sutton Coldfield Council Minutes for the Highways Committee for 1928-29 reported traffic problems at the Gravelly Lane and Boldmere Junction when they drew attention to the increase in accidents there and decided to erect four cross road signs with reflectors. They hoped this would alleviate the problem.

The middle aged woman wearing a flowery summer hat sits waiting in a car that must have been considered a mechanical wonder at the time. This was the sunny scene at the Old Jockey, Sutton Coldfield, many years ago.

At the same meeting it was recorded that no further decision had been made by the Ministry of Transport with regard to standardising road automatic signals.

The central standard at the junction of Chester and College Roads, one of the heavy pattern lamp standards with iron posts round it for protection, was erected on the refuge and fitted with a large candle-power light and red lamps, but was "knocked down by a lorry at about 3.30am on the 8th instant, clearing the site apparently without a great deal of damage to the vehicle as it went on and has not been traced".

Another was erected with wooden instead of iron posts to protect it. These posts were knocked down when run into a second time, but this time the posts protected the lamp. It was requested that a policeman be stationed at this point to direct the traffic.

The number of roads in Boldmere was increased at this time, 1929-30, with the making up of Britwell Road and Monmouth Drive, whilst in Gate Lane, one of Boldmere's oldest roads, houses numbered 33 to 39 were erected, as confirmed by the date plaque of "1928" set on the front of the houses. Near the entrance of Gate Lane are four houses which are apparently of much older origin, possibly of the Victorian era.

Family Life in Boldmere

Douglas V. Jones (1917-1991), a well known local historian, who lived in Boldmere from 1949, when he married, described in an article in the *Sutton News* on April 21st, 1989 his boyhood days in and around Boldmere, and how, long before The Boulevard, Sunnybank Road and New Church Road had been built, he would walk across the fields to Boldmere after passing under the railway bridge from Green Lanes.

——— This is how he describes the scene in his book ———

Memories of a Twenties Child

"We moved into No 39 Green Lanes in 1926.....

Beyond our garden there were fields extending to the railway embankment of the Sutton and Four Oaks branch line, strewn in summer with wild flowers, and beyond the railway, more fields as far as Boldmere Road. There was a pathway, spanned by a bridge, under the railway, used by the farmer and his men to take their carts and farm implements to and from fields on either side of the track. The level of the land had been lowered at this point and local boys always called the hollow 'Devil's Ditch'. which became a rendezvous and hide-out as well as a focal-point for a variety of activities. Train-spotting; cow-boys and Indians; tip-cat; five-stones; conkers and other diversions filled the wide-margined days of childhood."

The Sutton and Four Oaks branch line in 1932 showing 'Devil's Ditch' a rendezvous and hideout for small boys.   *Photo Douglas V. Jones*

Local Farming in the 1930s

At that time at the entrance to the future New Church Road was a five barred gate. The farmer and his men used the pathway spanned by the bridge to take their carts and farming implements to and from the fields on either side of the track.

He said farming methods in those days were very basic, and the ploughing and reaping were undertaken with the horse providing the power to activate the machinery, and how it was not unusual to see one farm labourer plant a whole field of potatoes by hand.

Harvest time was looked forward to by all the local children, for it was then they were able to earn some pocket money by collecting potatoes and gathering up the sheaves of golden grain as they spewed out of the machine. They then stacked them in stooks with seven or eight sheaves of wheat or barley to the stook, for there were no combine harvesters then.

One part of the job which the children enjoyed and which caused much excitement was when the reaping machine, working its way in from the perimeter of the field, reached the middle where the area of corn was reduced to a tiny rectangle of standing corn. There would then be a hasty exodus and frenzied scattering in all directions of rabbits, mice and voles as the last of their protective covering was cut away from them.

NEW ROADS BUILT

During the depression of the 1930s the Council, in an endeavour to provide some relief to the considerable unemployment which was endemic in Sutton

Traffic island at the junction of Stonehouse Road and Monmouth Drive.

69

and throughout the country, took advantage of the financial assistance provided by the Unemployment Grants Committee and employed local men to build roads and in so doing so created two new roads, Antrobus Road and Monmouth Drive. This not only helped to open up the area for further development, but provided work for men who would otherwise have been on the dole. It also contributed to the growth of Boldmere.

On the corner of Highbridge Road and Boldmere Road, on the opposite side to the Library, used to stand a sweet shop in which local children would spend their pocket money. It was a very dark little shop. Some favourite sweets for the children were "Little Imps", which were tiny liquorice sweets. They were popular because being so small they could eat them in class without being caught by teacher.

THE TWO BOLDMERE POST OFFICES

In the 1900 *Kellys Directory* Mr Robert Ball is shown as proprietor and is described as Grocer and Provision Dealer and Post Office. He was still there in 1924, for he is shown in *Kellys* of that year. Mr Ball's was the only Post Office in Boldmere until the 1890s, when the shops at the Erdington end of Boldmere Road were built and Mr Joseph Dunn, who was a Draper, took on the duties of Postmaster at the present address, 394 Boldmere Road, which in 1900 was not numbered. He was there for some years, but does not appear in the 1924 Directory.

By 1940 Mr Ball had gone and his Post Office was transferred to 86 Boldmere Road, the present *Granny Smith's* Greengrocer. Eventually this was moved to 15 Boldmere Road, its present address, but was identified as *Boldmere Post Office*, whereas number 394 Boldmere Road was called *Boldmere Road Post Office*, which in 1940 was run by Miss Rosalie Kathleen Page, Shopkeeper and Post Office. The Post Office still at 394 is called Boldmere Road Post Office to distinguish it from the office at 15 Boldmere Road which is called simply Boldmere Post Office.

Britwell Hall in Britwell Road was officially opened in 1933 by Miss Bertha Parkes, Mr Howard Cant and Mr H. R. Leach. The hall, which is attached to Wylde Green United Reform Church, cost £3,300 to build and can accommodate 300 people.

A Spate of House Building

The 1930s saw a spate of building in Boldmere. Some of the houses erected promised guaranteed unrestricted views of the park and cost £600.

Also in 1933 the Corporation built in Church Road a number of bungalows especially for the occupation of elderly couples of small means. They comprised one living room, a bedroom and bathroom etc.

In October 1936 in an endeavour to regulate and control the flow of traffic a traffic island was set up at the junction of Boldmere Road and Jockey Road. It made a decorative addition with its brightly planted flower beds.

A photograph taken in 1936 shows a notice board on the corner of Britwell Road and Highbridge Road advertising houses built on that site at £575 each. These houses, however, had something added to them which many houses around the district did not have. It was a brick built garage, which clearly demonstrated just how popular the motor car was becoming.

On the corner of Boldmere Road and Station Road one of the earliest houses to be built in Boldmere had now reached the stage where it was being demolished to make way for modern houses, for in 1938 a notice board was erected giving details of the "superior detached residences" to be built there.

They were to be offered for sale at £900 each, which in those days was a considerable sum for anyone to pay for a house. The builders were Newman & Co of Erdington. Other old properties in 1938 to fall to the demolisher's hammer were the *Gate Inn* and the adjacent cottages.

THE OLD GATE INN

The replacement for the *Gate Inn*, which in earlier days was advertised as *The Old Gayte Inn*, was the more modern and considerably larger *Boldmere Inn*, whose date of erection can still be seen on the rainwater heads.

When the *Gate Inn* was built in the mid 1800s the usual means of transport for its customers was by foot, horseback or horse and cart. By 1939 times had changed considerably and the Inn, now in a built up area and not isolated in

country surroundings, needed to be brought up to date. So the new *Boldmere Inn*, instead of being right on the corner of Gate Lane and Boldmere Road, was set well back from Boldmere Road, leaving ample room in front of the building for a substantial car park.

Over the years in an endeavour to keep itself up to date, considerable sums of money have been spent renovating and updating the *Boldmere*. Today, however, it has, after extensive alterations, changed its name to *The Harvester*.

The Harvester (formerly The Boldmere Hotel)
on the corner of Gate Lane and Boldmere Road.

TROUBLE WITH THE DRAINS

Problems with draining away surface water still existed in Boldmere in 1936, so the Council invited tenders for the construction of a surface water sewer in Stonehouse Road and Boldmere Road, comprising approximately 500 yards of concrete and stoneware pipes, bricks and manholes. Two years later in 1938 the Sanitary Authority resolved to construct a sewer, pave, metal, flag, channel and make good and provide proper means for lighting parts of the New Church Road from Boldmere Road for a distance of 245 yards.

POWELL'S POOL INCORPORATED INTO THE PARK

Powell's Pool came into the possession of the Corporation in 1937 and so became part of the park, plus a piece of land on the perimeter of the park. This was conveyed from the Somerville Trust.

In 1939 applications were invited for the tenancy of the shop at the Boldmere entrance to Sutton Park. A tender was accepted to carry out improvements to *Powell's Pool* to the extent of £4,798. This included erecting a cafe, boathouse and shops.

NEW BOLDMERE SCHOOLS ERECTED

To cater for the growth in private dwelling houses and the consequent growth in population, the original Girls and Infants School built in 1848 needed replacing, so in 1938 the new Boldmere Schools to accommodate Senior Boys, Senior Girls, Juniors and Infants were erected in Cofield and St Michael's Roads. Enrolment for the very first influx of children took place on August 31st, 1938. The new schools were officially opened in October 1938. Mr Chapman was Head of the Senior Boys and Miss Barton, Head of the Senior Girls.

For some years single decker buses had run through Sutton Coldfield, but in 1939 this was to change when, after agreement with Sutton Coldfield Council, the Midland Red Bus Company agreed to run double deckers to Sutton from Birmingham, passing down Jockey Road and through Boldmere.

A criticism of Sutton's signposting was raised by a correspondent in the *Sutton News* in 1939, when he pointed out that strangers alighting from the bus in Jockey Road invariably had to ask the way to Sutton Park, even though they might be on the corner of Jockey Road and Stonehouse Road, for there was not a signpost at all giving directions to Sutton Park, an anomaly the correspondent thought needed rectifying considering the Boldmere entrance to the park was the second most used entrance after Town Gate.

World War II

The year 1939 was a most ominous year for this was when, in September, the fears of most people were realised: War with Germany was declared. In October the Government made available to the public at varying prices Anderson Air Raid Shelters.

Jockey Road bomb damage being repaired in 1941, the bomb dropped in front of Jennings Garage, now Rydale.

Many people in Boldmere bought these air raid shelters and set them up in their gardens. They were available for cash or payment in instalments. For the large family or a group of neighbours a shelter accommodating ten people cost £10.18s.0d; for eight people £9.12s.0d; for six people £8.0s.0d; and for four people £6.19s.0d. After serving the population for the duration of the War many of these corrugated steel Anderson shelters existed for years, being used for a variety of purposes. There may well be one or two existing in some Boldmere back gardens even today.

BOLDMERE AMBULANCE STATION

The original Girls and Infants School built in 1848 was requisitioned for the War and used as an Ambulance Station, with many local women being recruited to drive the ambulances. After the War the School was used for evening classes but today it is used as a clinic.

At the Boldmere end of the park the Civil Defence Camp was converted to a National Fire Service Training School and later, in 1948, was given a new lease of life as a European Volunteer Workers Hostel, which brought many Latvians and Lithuanians to the district.

Alderman H. B. Brassington aged 74 died in 1942. He was one of the founder members of the Boldmere and Wylde Green Conservative Club, which opened on the 26th April 1913. He was the first Librarian during the 1914-18 War and encouraged swimming by his continued support of the Boldmere Swimming Club, whose annual general meetings were held at the *Sutton Park Hotel*. He was a member of Sutton Coldfield Town Council as one of the representatives for the Boldmere Ward.

A Second World War view of the National Fire Service Camp, overlooking Powell's Pool.

RABBIT CATCHING PERMITS ISSUED

During those austere times when just about everything was either in short supply or on ration, one concession granted by the Corporation and welcomed by all, was being allowed to take rabbits from the park (long before myxamatosis affected the rabbit population).

Guns were not allowed to be used, and anyone digging out the rabbits was under an obligation to fill and level the holes after the rabbits were taken.

At Boldmere any resident within the Borough could obtain a permit to authorise them to take rabbits in the park on the 15th and 22nd of February between 8am and 5pm. Permits were obtained on application to the Park Forester at the main gate, or from the various gatekeepers, including the keeper at Boldmere Gate.

Houses in Stonehouse Road built after earlier properties were destroyed by
a German Bomb dropped in rear gardens in 1942.

Postwar Development

Most of Boldmere had been developed by the 1930s before the commencement of the Second World War, but one thoroughfare still to be developed after the War was Monmouth Drive. A photograph taken in 1949 by S.A. Jeavons shows Monmouth Drive looking from Banners Gate. with not a house in sight.

The time had arrived for *Stonehouse Farm* to be pulled down. It was the 1950s and a photograph taken just prior to demolition shows the farm to be of substantial brick built construction with tall farm buildings enclosing a farmyard. The buildings would house cattle, farm machinery and implements. Outside the side door of the farmhouse stood an old hand-cranked water pump which provided the domestic water supply. All this was now to disappear and today in its place on the corner of Corbridge Road and Stonehouse Road stands a modern bungalow.

One of the farmers, Mr Austin Chipman had, during the War, heeded the exhortations of the Government to "Dig for Victory", for in 1944 he, together with many other local people, exhibited some of their produce at the Allotment Committee's Third Show in the Town Hall. His entries were in the commercial section of the show for he exhibited a fine crop of *Arran Banner* potatoes and the correct method of straw clamping.

Scale of 1 Mile

LONGMOOR POOL

POWELLS POOL

DRIFFOLD

Old Park Farm

Hosp.

Sch.

NEW OSCOTT

St. Mary's R.C. College

BOLDMERE

STA.

Boldmere Street Map c.1956/7.

Note land at either end of Monmouth Drive
had not yet been developed for housing.

STA

CHESTER ROAD

St Nicholas R.C. Church Erected

March 1953 saw the opening of the new Roman Catholic Church of St Nicholas in Jockey Road, replacing the little chapel in Boldmere Road, which was also dedicated to St Nicholas and built over one hundred years earlier to serve the spiritual needs of the small Catholic community of the rural district of Sutton Coldfield.

The new Church, costing £18,000 to build, provided accommodation for 300 worshippers and was built in the Romanesque style. Because of building restrictions it was not possible at that time to complete the building scheme. The nave still needed to be lengthened and the narthex to be added.

Booths Farm was another old landmark to go in the 1950s. This was on a section of the Somerville Estate, where two roads were laid out. The Highways Committee agreed that they should be named Denholm Road and Stirling Road.

Most of the buildings on the even side of Boldmere Road have escaped re-development so the original Victorian frontages remain as this detail shows.

THE PEOPLE VERSUS THE COUNCIL

One Boldmere couple was, in 1954, having housing problems and difficulty with the Council. They were Mr and Mrs W. K. Warren. Apparently Mr Warren was discharged from the army in 1949 for health reasons and at the time was advised by his doctor to live in a hut.

Following the doctor's advice he found such a property behind number 395 Jockey Road. It was a hut measuring 14 feet by 6 feet 9 inches and stood on a solid brick and concrete base and there both he and his wife lived, raising a family of three children, who at that time in 1954 were aged five, two and a baby.

His problem with the Council was that they alleged his hut was unfit for habitation and was overcrowded. The accusation was made by the Senior Sanitary Inspector to the Borough, and as a result of his action a demolition order was placed on the hut and the family given 27 days to vacate the place. Mr and Mrs Warren refused to comply with the order so the Corporation applied for a Warrant of Possession, which was granted by the Court and which authorised forcible ejection of the occupants by the police.

Mr Warren told the Bench, ''I've done nothing wrong at all''. He protested, ''All I've done is live in a shed. Nobody could have bonnier kids than I've got. Where can I go?'' As nothing had been mentioned about the family being rehoused, presumably they would be homeless.

Another person having problems with the Council was a butcher who had applied to them to use his Boldmere Road premises as a slaughterhouse. Alderman H. A. Hothersall objected saying, ''I think it unwise to have such a place in a densely populated area as Boldmere''.

The butcher was not put off by the Council's objections and took his appeal against the Council's refusal to grant him a licence to the Appeals Committee of the Warwickshire Quarter Sessions. The Appeals Committee overruled the Council and granted the butcher his licence, much to the annoyance of the Council.

MORE PROBLEM DRAINS

Drainage in Boldmere still continued to plague the Council for, in 1955, the most costly item on the Highways Committee's estimates was the Boldmere Drainage Scheme estimated at £150,000, to be carried out in a four year period beginning in 1956, whilst still in 1955 steps were being taken to alleviate flooding in Britwell Road.

The Scouts Jamboree of 1957

An event of international importance took place in Sutton Park, when for 12 days from the 1st to the 12th August, 1957 32,000 Scouts from 87 parts of the World held the World Jamboree of the Scout movement, which was opened by H.R.H. The Duke of Gloucester. For weeks before the event activity in setting up the various facilities for the Scouts was intense.

The Boldmere area was affected by the extra traffic travelling to and from the park through the Boldmere entrance carrying supplies and equipment to the gigantic camp. Within a short time of the arrival of all the Scouts, they settled themselves in, erecting tents and establishing their own country's territory which residents in Boldmere and elsewhere could visit.

The Scouts were not confined to the park so the shopkeepers and people of Boldmere were entertained by the myriad of foreign languages being spoken as the Scouts either window-gazed or did their shopping.

A ROYAL VISIT

On 3rd August the Queen and Prince Philip paid a visit to the Jamboree, an event enjoyed by all.

Another event, which was totally unexpected and most unwelcome, was a terrific storm which unleashed itself over Sutton, flooding the camp to such an extent that many Scouts had to move in to Church Halls, Schools and private houses.

The residents of Sutton, including those in Boldmere, opened their hearts to the Scouts in their sad plight, offering help and assistance. The Scouts were not downhearted and set to to clear up the mess. Soon, everything was restored to good order.

People travelled from all around the Midlands and the country to the park, and Boldmere for those twelve days was able to share in the excitement and enjoyment of such a major international event.

More Demolition of Old Boldmere

Demolition of some of the old buildings continued apace. The next one to go was the *Station Inn* on the corner of Highbridge Road and Boldmere Road. This had provided a stopping off place for locals and park visitors since the

The corner of Highbridge Road and Boldmere Road in the 1950s. Boldmere Library, shops and maisonettes were built at this junction in 1960.

1880s. Replacing it was another building designed to provide a useful service to the people of Boldmere. It was a full time Branch Library which was built in 1960.

Other buildings to be demolished were those adjacent to the *Sutton Park Inn* and continuing up to the Branch Library. These were replaced by modern blocks of shops. Later, in the 1960s, came the block containing the Post Office. Up the adjacent passage-way behind the new shops, you arrive at an open area, created when a number of old bungalows which had stood there since the 1800s were taken down. This open area is now used as a car park.

There were protests when the question of multi-storey flats being built in Boldmere was raised. It was proposed they be erected at the junction of Boldmere Road and Firtree Grove. In spite of the protests and charges of "great

First block of Municipal multi-storey flats, Park Court, Boldmere Road, officially opened 28th April 1964.

ugly monstrosities looming out of the sky" building went ahead and so the first multi-storey flats in Sutton Coldfield were built in Boldmere.

Fire Destroys St Michael's Church

One of Boldmere's oldest buildings was in July 1964 almost destroyed by fire. it was St Michael's Church, which had been built in 1857. The fire started

St Michaels Church which was severely damaged by fire in 1964.

in the early hours of the morning and the roof was soon ablaze from end to end. Firemen from two brigades, Warwickshire and Birmingham, were in attendance. The Church was gutted, but a rebuilt Church rose from the ashes in 1967. It was built in a modern style when it was found it could not be reconstructed in its original form. It was consecrated in 1967 by Dr J. L. Wilson, late Bishop of Birmingham.

JOCKEY ROAD WIDENING

Jockey Road was widened in 1967 and as a result 150 houses lost part of their front gardens. Nearby, 56 acres of farm land at New Oscott, described as the last of the large plots of land in Sutton, was sold for £685,000 to build 350 homes on the site fronting onto Chester Road North.

Some 45 acres of land from the Somerville Estate between Monmouth Drive and Stonehouse Road had been, since 1961, in the course of development. *Stonehouse Farm* had gone and the farm tenant had occupied premises once known as *Jockey Lane Farm Cottage*.

Now it was the turn of the traffic island, which stood close by *Wrights the Bakers* on the corner of Jockey Road and Boldmere Road, to be removed, for

The junction of Boldmere Road and Jockey Road taken about 1963.

in July 1970 it was replaced by a set of automatic traffic signals to ease the congestion.

At the same time, a curved protrusion was added to the pavement opposite the Post Office, where a bus shelter and stop now are. It was intended to divide a parking bay from what was a slip road into Jockey Road. Local people called it a "bump". The Surveyor's Department said it was a "nib", and motorists called it a "hazard". It is still there today and provides a convenient parking area for motorists. Similar parking places have since been created along Boldmere Road.

An Arsonist Strikes!

A spate of arsonist attacks had occurred in 1972 causing damage and destruction in various places throughout the town. The shop next door to Wylde Green Station fell victim to such an attack, which caused severe damage. Another incident took place early one morning in August 1972, when *La Reserve*, the lakeside night club at *Powell's Pool* near Boldmere Gate, was victim of the arsonist.

A policeman quickly on the scene summoned assistance and called the Fire Brigade, which wasted no time getting there. The policeman also saw a man running off into nearby woods so the park was sealed off and all exits closed.

Whilst the firemen tackled the blaze, a massive manhunt by sixty policemen was undertaken, but in spite of the man being seen to break cover he managed to give the police the slip within the vast area of parkland and escaped.

Two boathouses and a store were destroyed by fire, which was started when a window was broken and burning material pushed through. *La Reserve* was due to re-open after a three week closure for extensions, and Mr Malcolm Dent, the Managing Director of the Club, said that in spite of the fire attack the Club would still open on time.

SUTTON PARK GATES A BLOW TO BOLDMERE TRADERS

Gates within Sutton Park were introduced in 1975. This was to cause problems with the small traders of Boldmere. Until the gates were introduced residents of Streetly had a direct run in their cars through the park to the Boldmere shopping area, which was much appreciated by the shopkeepers of Boldmere, who enjoyed a reasonable trade with them.

With the gates in the park now being closed, this effectively stopped the straight run through the park, so it became inconvenient for the Streetly residents to make a detour with the resultant adverse effect on trade as the shopping went elsewhere. In spite of protests the gates have remained in place.

This raised another query with the Boldmere Traders' Association. There were no signposts directing people to the Boldmere Shopping Centre and it was suggested at their annual meeting that approaches be made to Birmingham City Council Engineering Department for Boldmere to be signposted to attract passing trade. Although perhaps the smaller shops could not compete with the larger stores in Sutton and Birmingham, they could offer the personal touch, which was not to be found at a supermarket. All the shops were at ground level, which was important for elderly people who did not like travelling to Birmingham.

'MOSES' FOUND IN BOLDMERE KIOSK

In June 1975 local people were shocked when a baby was found abandoned in a telephone kiosk in Boldmere. A 67 year old grandmother found the baby hidden in a brown carrier bag. The police were called and the baby taken to *Good Hope Hospital*, where the nurses nicknamed him "Moses". After many appeals and attempts to trace the mother she was never found and "Moses" went to foster parents. Today the baby, wherever he is and whatever his eventual new parents decided to name him, will be a young adult.

SMOKE CONTROL INTRODUCED

Over 500 homes in Boldmere became affected by the new smoke controlled area from July 1st 1976. From that date householders were only allowed to burn solid smokeless fuels and the cost to Birmingham City Council of adapting and replacing fireplaces was £2,925. The new smokeless zone covered 117 acres and is bounded by Station Road on the North, from its junction with Boldmere

Road, to the junction with the Birmingham-Sutton railway line. Its eastern limit follows the railway and the western limit is a portion of Chester Road North.

Clarkes Transport Ltd of Gate Lane decided in June 1978 to close the gully between numbers 50 and 52 Britwell Road into Gate Lane following an increase in vandalism. Local people were upset at the gully being blocked off because it meant a much longer walk to get to the shops, but they were in fact relieved by the closure because of the vandalism. Mr Peter Carr, Company Director, said he was making moves to put gates at either end of the passage and if any elderly people would like a key they could apply to him.

HARVESTER STAFF PARACHUTE FOR CHARITY

At the entrance to Gate Lane today stands the *Harvester* public house. In 1980 it was still called the *Boldmere Public House* and from newspaper reports its staff expressed their desire to help a charity in a way that most of us would consider too dangerous. Some of the staff of the *Harvester* were among seven men and three women who volunteered to parachute from a Cesna 205 light aircraft at Halfpenny Green Airport to help raise funds for leukæmia research.

ONE WAY SCHEME FOR SHEFFIELD ROAD

Sheffield Road was in the news in July 1981, when the West Midlands Highways Committee put forward a one-way scheme to try to alleviate problems caused by cars parking on both sides of Sheffield Road. It was proposed it should run from Boldmere Road, along Sheffield Road and Marston Road into Chester Road. Many residents said it should run the other way. To support this view, Mr Paul Wakelin of Chester Road and Mrs Muriel Lander, Acting Secretary of Sheffield Road Residents Association, had collected over 60 signatures for their petition. Mr Wakelin said the scheme should run the other way or be scrapped.

He said it would be very difficult to turn into Chester Road, particularly to turn right, and he warned it could cause some accidents. People leaving the *Cork and Bottle* Wine Bar after a few drinks would present the greatest risk. County Councillor Michael Wilcox said the emergency services favoured the present direction of the scheme. He did not feel strongly either way, but would give his support to the petitioners.

In March 1982 the Council said the one-way traffic system would soon be implemented if the residents agreed with the West Midlands County Council proposals that the traffic travel towards the Chester Road.

BOLDMERE ROAD IN 1959

Boldmere Road Shops and Businesses, together with private residences, as listed in the *Sutton Coldfield Directory* published at 15/- (fifteen shillings which in today's money would be 75p) by Kent Services Ltd. of London.

BOLDMERE ROAD
(Jockey Road to Chester Road)
Left Side
1 Park Hotel (P.H.)
Lic.: Allen, T.
St. Nicholas Church Hall (R.C.)
17 Wimbush, Ambrose & Son—Conftnrs.
17 Ashford, J. H.
19 Payne, H. H. Ltd.— Footwear Repairs
21 Willetts, Miss D. E. —Upholsterer
23 Matthews, J. W.— Wines & Spirits
23 (rear) Cooke, W. H.
23 (rear) Kneller, A. J.
25 Price's Stores (Price, H. C.)—Groc. & Pr.
25 (rear) Bond, Mrs. E. M.
29 Beadmans Ltd.— Butchers
31/33 Saunders (S. Cldfield) Ltd.—Frnshrs.
35/35a Edward Rose (B'ham) Ltd.—

37 Butler, Walter— Florist
45 Smith, L. P.
49 Rickards, Frank— Motor Cycles, Cycles & Scooters
51 Fleetwood, E. W.— Butcher
53 "Delicatessen"— Cooked Meats (Fleetwood, E. W.)

Union Drive here—
55 Vogue—Ladies Gowns (Smallwood, Mrs. M. E.)
57 Boldmere Eletricity Service Centre— M.E.B.

Queens Chambers
1 Arthur Overton & Co. Ltd.—Turf Accounts
2/3 W. H. Heywood & Co. Ltd.—Patent Glazing & Thermal Installations
2/3 Helliwell & Co. Ltd.—Patent Glazing & Metal Windows

4 J. L. Robbins— Manfng. Furrier
5/6 Betts Partners (V. D. Betts, D. E. Trist) —Office & Stationery Supplies
7/9 Nail Boxes Ltd.
10 ——
11 Maurice Ashby Ltd. —Pigment Manfrs.
12 G. G. Thompson— Engineering Tracing

59 Bayliss & Co. Ltd. — Builders' Mchts.

Gate Lane here—
Boldmere Hotel (Lic.: Cale, C. A. E.)
83 Williams, W. L.
85 Swain, Mrs. E.
87 Dickinson, Mrs. D. E.
89 Leeson, W. W. G.
91 Higginson, R.
93 Mason, L. J.
95 Pugh, Mrs. F. E.
97 Hand, Miss M. C. R.
99 Flint, V. R.
101 Haddon, F.

Bayliss & Co's showroom on the corner of Gate Lane in the 1930s — now occupied by Barretts.

103 Smith, A. W. J.
105 Lee, H. J.
107 Thompson, W. J.
109 Goodall, W. H.
111 Cherrington, A.

Fir Tree Grove
1 Johnston, W. J.
2 Jones, E.
3 Coursh, B. A.
4 Herbert, W. J.

———

Boldmere Rd. contd.—
Highbridge Rd. here—
121 ——
123 ——
125 Taylor, Miss H. A.
127 Gill, Mrs. A. J.
129 Colonius, Miss A.M.
131 Gunston, Mrs. R.
133 Moss, T. A.
135 Harris, J. D.
137 Sprason, N. M.
139 Cooksey, A.
141 Trevelyan,
          Mrs. F. A.
143 Williams, H. K.
145 Richardson, J. W.
147 Pearce, J. O.
149 Moseley, W. A.
151 Brough, H. J. W.
153 Portsmouth, H. S.
153 Jackson, Dr. W. M.
          M.B., B.Ch.
155 Edwards, F.
157 Webb, R. J.
159 Habak, M.
161 Hadley, H. O.
163 Barron, W. R. T.
165 Lowe, N. J. J.
167 Rice & Styche—
          Pntrs., Decrs. &
          Domestic Engrs.
167 Rice, G. J.
169 Stokes, Mrs. D. E.
171 Rice, P. B.
173 Knightley, H. A.
175 Randall, Mrs. M. E.
177 Warburton,
          Mrs. L. A.
179 Bayliss, Mrs. D.
185 Keenan, H. —
          Monumental Mason
187 Holyoake,
          Miss G. A.
189 Gracey, G. V.
191 Gracey, A. A.

Beacon Rd. here—

203 Morris, S. J.
205 Thomas, G.
207 Parsons, C. J.
209 Jones, Mrs. F.
211 Hicks, T.

213 Gregg, H. W.
215 Lavender, A.
217 Kempton, C. A.
219 Blumfield, Miss N.
221 Gilbert, S. G. B.
223 Cotterill, L. H.
225 Sawyer, R. C.

Station Road here—
233 Rowe, P. E.
235 Chamberlain, C.
237 Dipple, J. A.
239 Chamberlain,
          Mrs. M. A.
239aWinters, G. R.
241 Arnold, D. G.

New Church Rd. here—
247 Thompson, W. G.
249 ——
251 Platt, G. W.
253 Hudson, A. P.
255 Pryce, G. A.
257 Baum, Miss C. A.
261 Alldrick, D. F.
263 Whitehouse, G. W.
265 French, T.
267 Brookes, A. E.
269 Potrac, J.
271 Hynes, L. J.

Sunny Bank Rd. here—
277 Lowe, W. R.
279 Jones, L. C.
281 Tasker, J. A.
283 McKenna, T. J.
285 Smith, T. P.
287 Green, Mrs. M. A.
289 Trafford,
          Mrs. E. L. A.

Boldmere Drive here—
291 McLaughlin, I. V.
293 Wassall, W. E.
295 French, T. G.
311 Drewry, A. A.
317 Nicholson, J.
319 Bolton,
          Misses, V. M. & D. J.
321 Underwood, P. S.
323 Sparkes, H. V.
323aDarkes, H.
323bThompson, A. J.
325 Gregory, R. J.—
          Nurseryman

Tube Investments Ltd.—
          Sports Ground &
          Pavilion
339 Smets, G.

341 Sturdy, E. J.
343 Pearson, J.
345 Stratford, Mrs. A. A.

347 Eades, Mrs. A. E.
349 Burrows, Mrs. E.
351 Allen, Miss E. M.
353 Hodgkinson,
          Mrs. M. H.
355 Whitfield, Mrs. E. C.
357 Kearsey, Miss G. M.
357aJohnson, Mrs. G. G.

Boldmere Close here—
359 Marston, G.—Groc.
          and Confectionery
361 Lee, W. A.
363 Hart, C. F.— G'gcr.
365 Smith, J. W.—Off
          License (Ansells
          Brewery Ltd.)

Sheffield Road here—
367 Keey, N. D.—Radio
          and T.V.
369 Thompson, N.
369 Payne, H. H. Ltd.—
          Footwear Repairs
371 Rowan, G. H.—
          Tob., Conftr. &
          Fancy Goods
373 Fletcher, F. N.
375 Wright, B.
377 Higgins, H. S.
379 Tonsley, A.
381 Douglas, P. J.
383 Hollingsworth,
          Mrs. E.
385 Fox, H.
387 Francis, J.
389 Whittaker, T. A.
391 Ottaway, H. V.
393 Oakes, W.
395 Flatman, F.
397 Brettell, S. J.
399 Hanley, M.
401 Kearne, T. E.
403 Reinprecht, J.
405 Richards, W.
407 Lewis, Mrs. E. C.

Boldmere Rd.—contd.

Right Side
2 Astons Stores (Ald-
          ridge) Ltd., ("As-
          tons")—Bakers and
          Confectioners
4 Roden, W. H., MPS
          —Chemist
6 Wrensons (Stores)
          Ltd.—Grcrs. & Prv.
6 Clack, L. J.
8 Cooper, G. H.
          —Dpr. & Ladies
          Outfitters

8 (Back) Kershaw,
　　　　　J. A.
10 Moore, Chris. C. —
　　Ironmonger
12 Innis, W. & Son —
　　G'grocery & Fish
　　(W. Innis)
14 Birmingham Co-op.
　　Soc. Ltd.—Grocery
16 Smith, A. J.
16 J. Green, Ltd. —
　　Greengrocery
18 Pearson, Norman F.
　　Ltd.—Elec. Equip-
　　ment, Radio, etc.
18 (Fl.) Blood, R.
20 Mason, Geo. J. Ltd.
　　—Grocers
22 Hunt, R. C.
22 Matthews, S.—Btchr.
24 Crofts, Mrs. E.
26 Clayton, A. E.
28 Yeomans, Mrs. E.
30 Allen, H. C.
32 **Fell, H. J. & Harper,**
　　F.A.I.—Chartered
　　Auctioneers & Estate
　　Agents, Surveyors &
　　Valuers
34 Chawner, C. E.
36 Groves, J.
38 Palmer, A. J.
40 Richards, W. (Aston)
　　Ltd.—Butchers
40 Kennemore, A. E.
42/4 Lampert (Paper-
　　hangings) Ltd.—
　　Wallpapers & Paints
46 Fitz-Gerald,
　　　　　Mrs. N. H.
46 Cafe Sunshine
　　　　(Mrs. Fitzgerald)

Redacre Road here—
52 The Cosy Cafe
　　(Mrs. F. M. Clarke)
52 Clarke, G. S.
54 Boldmere Cleaners—
　　Dry Cleaners
56 Mather, V. E.
58 Warwick Library
　　(F. C. Wareham)—
　　Lending Library
60 Burgess, Miss E. D.
60aDenise (Mrs. M. Eve)
　　—Gen. Drapery
62 Harris, Joseph, Ltd.
　　—Dry Cleaners &
　　Dyers

64 Kings of Boldmere
　　Ltd.—Toys

66 Wm. C. Miller,
　　F.B.O.A., Dip.Opt.—
　　Ophthalmic Optician

68 Hardy, Ann —
　　Millinery
70 Jones, P. J.
72 Jones, L. T.
74 Taylor, G. R.
76 Cross, H.
78 Hitchman, T.—
　　Butcher
80 Boldmere Post Office
　　—Stnrs., News &
　　Tob. (Roberts, P. E.)
80 Barnhurst, F. C.
82 John Frost (Bold-
　　mere) Ltd.—Disp.
　　Chemist & Photo-
　　graphics
82 (Fl) Larcombe, D. F.
84/6 Chamberlains
　　(Sutton Coldfield)
　　Ltd.—G'gcr. & Fruit
84 (Fl.) Swain, A. W.
86 Groves, H. L.
88 Lightfoot, C. H.—
　　Footwear Repairs
88aLyons, Miss J. H.
90 Midland Bank Ltd.
92 Boldmere Drapery
　　(Humpage, G. R.)
92aBrisbourne, P. L. Y.
92aGordon, Vera—
　　Ladies' Outfitters
　　(Mrs. J. Brisbourne)
92bBate, H.—Corn &
　　Seed Merchant
94 Barrett, A. E. & O.
　　R.—Toys, Sweets &
　　Tobacco
94 Barrett, A. E.
96 Lea, Mrs. H. D.
96 **Hilda Walker—**
　　(Mrs. H. D. Lee)—
　　Wools & Knitwear,
　　Baby's & Children's
　　Wear, Ladies',
　　Gent's & Children's
　　Outfitters
98 Maison Sorrell—
　　Ladies' Hrdrsr.
　　(A. J. Evans)
98 Evans, A. J.
100 Harrison, B. A.—
　　Grocer
102 Watts, L. J.
104 Scown, G. H.
Boldmere Hall Social
　　Club
Boldmere Methodist
　　Church (Rev. J. D.
　　Cape)
Sutton Coldfield Corp. Br
　　Lib. (Boldmere Br.)

110 Gills School of
　　Motoring
110 Forder, J. T.
112 Hilton, E. H.
114 Kelly, J. P.
116 Downey, L. V.
118 Com-Tele (Birming-
　　ham) Co. Ltd.—
　　Radio & T.V.
118 (Fl.) Morgan, J. P.
120 Wrensons (Stores)
　　Ltd.—Gcy. & Provs.
120 (Fl.) Scott, R.

Antrobus Rd. here—
144 Wilwear Shoe Rprs.
　　(H. W. Sadler)
144 Sadler, H. W.
146 E. & N. Beech—
　　Gent's Hairdresser
148 Thomas, H. J.
150 Pearson, T.
152 Cash, J. T.
154 Washbourne, W. D.
156 Fitzpatrick, R. S.
158 Ashcroft, Miss A.
160 Kay, H. H.
162 Carter, R.
164 Webster, W. E.
166 Laughton, Mrs. E. E.
168 Evans, F. J.
170 Bates, Miss E. F.
172 Robinson, D. H.

Cofield Road here—
182 Smith, Mrs. M.
184 Stephens, Mrs. N.
186 Stephens, G. N.
188 Newton, F.
190 G. T. Stephens &
　　Sons Ltd.—Building
　　Contrs. (Office &
　　Yard)
192 Boldmere Parish
　　Church Council (St.
　　Michael's Parish
　　Rooms)
192 (rear) 1st Sutton
　　Coldfield Scouts HQ
194 Warwicks County
　　Council—Boldmere
　　Clinic & Ambulance
　　Depot & School
　　Meals Centre
196 Payne, Miss A. E.
198 Whitehouse, Mrs. E.

St. Michael's Road here
212 Jackson, L.
214 Mudd, Miss P. M.
216 Leigh, A. F.
218 Thompson, L.
220 Maitland, J. S.

222 Stiff, Miss E. G.
224 Riley, W. F.
226 Williams, S. M.
228 (Flats)—
    1 Kirby, E. W.
    2 Reynolds, R. G.

Church Road here—
252 Bedford, S. A.
254 Davis, F. A.
256 Watson, W. G.
258 Barnett, G. V.
260 Anderson, J. G.
262 Dawson, T. T.
264 Bashford, Mrs. R. W.
266 Withers, R.
268 McAllum, Rev. J. C.
270 Wignell, S. E.
272 Low, H. C.
274 Peel, E. A.
276 (Flats)—
    1 Yates, W. H.
    2 Yates, C. J.
    3 Dickworth, H. J.
278 Tracey, W.
288 Highfield Nursing
    Home (Matron: Mrs.
    A. G. Southworth),
    C.N., S.R.N.
290 Moore, T. W.
292 Smith, Mrs. M. R.
294 Stephens, Mrs. E.
300 Dobbs, J. S.
302 Broadribb, A. H.
304 Abell, R. B.
306 Jones, Mrs. E.
314 Nock, Mrs. E.

316 Jones, R. P.
318 Cooke, G.
320 Whitefield, C. G. G.
322 Horton, M. V.
324 Horton, A. W. V.
326 (Flats)—
    1 Beale, R. C.
    2 Woolams,
             Mrs. M. E.
    3 Smith, Mr.
    4 Cahill, J/F.
328 Webber, D. C.
330 Spears, J. A.
332 (Flats)—
    1 Watson, P. H.
    2 Brewster. J. W.
334 Venables, A.
336 Jones, W. F.
338 North Birmingham
    Bridge Club
340 Grace, F. B. W.
342 Beddard, Mrs. B. E.
344 Ridge, W. J.
346 Wainwright, H. C.
348 Chapman, C. H.
350 Shiers, A. J.
352 Evans, A. G.
354 (Flats)—
    1 Cleal, C.
    2 Avery, R. J.
356 (Flats)—
    1 Evans, C. B.
    2 Watson, A.
358 Bant, Miss E. E.
366 Webb, J.—Tobcnst.
368 ——

370 "Florence"—Hair
    Stylist
372 ——
374 ——
376 Ridley, Mrs. M.—
    G'grocer & Florist
378 Blake's—Ironmngrs.,
    Hware, China &
    Glass Merchants
380 Bolton, A. E.
380 Ridgway, W. T.,
    M.P.S.—Chemist
382 Newbold, A. E.
382 Allsop, J.—Butcher
384 Bird, W. J.—Gcry.,
    Bakers & Confec.
386 Preece, E. G.
386 Webber, D. C.—
    Gents Outfitter
388 The Paint Pot—
    Paints & Wallpapers
    (Cobbold, A. A.)
388 (Flats)—
    1 Dougall, R. C.
    2 Coleyshaw, A. J.
390 Pilkington, D. H.
390 Page, Mrs. D.—
    Ladies' Outfitter
392 Felton, J. H.—Stnr.,
    News & Tobacco
394 Usher, F. S.
394 Boldmere Post Office
Chester Road Baptist
    Church Scnoolroom
Chester Rd. Baptist Ch.
    (Rev. P. Jones)

The Pavillion Cinema which used to face the junction of Boldmere Road and Chester Road. Before being demolished it was converted to Ten Pin Bowling which extended its life for several years. Part of the site is now occupied by housing.

Corner of Boldmere Road and Jockey Road.

Shopping and Business in Boldmere

Number 2 Boldmere Road is a double-fronted building standing on the corner of Boldmere Road and Jockey Road with its large windows displaying its goods and services in each road. It stands opposite the *Sutton Park Hotel* and over the years has housed a variety of businesses.

Sara J. Tustin in 1940 was described as a baker. She was followed by Wrights, Bakers and Confectionary. An estate agent took over in 1981 when city planners gave the go-ahead for the conversion of the premises into an estate agents office when Richard D. Parker of Four Oaks applied for planning permission. No objections to change of use were received, although City Planner, Mr Graham Shaylor, said application was refused twice before on the grounds that the unit should be used for shopping because of its prominent position.

Today, in 1993, it is occupied by Cornerstone Estate Agents, which belongs to the Abbey National Building Society.

All the shops on Boldmere Road have had quite a turnover of occupiers, trades and businesses. Next door at Number 4 Boldmere Road in 1940 was William Howard Roden, Chemist, then Wrensons, Grocers at Number 6; Harry Paget, Draper No 8; Chris C. Moore, Ironmonger No 10; W. Innis & Son, Fruiterer No 12; Birmingham Co-operative Society No 13; Wm Cooke, another Fruiterer No16; Norman Pearson, Electrical Engineer No 18; George Mason, part of a well-known chain of grocers No 20; Sidney Matthews, Butcher No 22; whilst at number 24 was Miss Miriam Crofts, teacher of music.

These are just a few of the dozens of shops in Boldmere recorded in the 1940 edition of *Kellys Directory*.

FAST FOOD BRINGS PROBLEMS

As can happen when a community grows, the more people that move in so more services that are required to meet their demands spring up. One of the modern businesses which, although a welcome addition, can bring its own problems with it, is that of the modern fast food take-away.

It was a sign of the times when in February 1982 the residents living in and around Fir Tree Grove and some nearby shopkeepers had reason to complain of a state of affairs that was causing some considerable annoyance.

Apparently a take-away food shop was attracting customers who would stand or sit around Fir Tree Grove consuming their food, and instead of disposing of their empty containers and waste paper into litter bins would throw them to the floor making the area very untidy. At lunch time school children were using Fir Tree Grove as a smoking parlour and eating take-away food there.

City Environmental Officer, Mr Harold Mitchell, said vandalism was a serious problem, but the Council could do little about it but promised to look at the problems caused by overturned bins.

MORE FLATS SQUEEZED IN

Most of the building land in Boldmere had been used up, but one builder found some space in a cul-de-sac off Chester Road where he could build some flats. It was Firsholm Close, which backed on to some houses in Boldmere Road. This was opposed by the people in Boldmere Road whose back gardens would be overlooked by the proposed 10 two-storey flats, 10 garages and 18 parking spaces, besides which they would lose trees and sunshine. In spite of their objections, the Birmingham Planning Committee granted the builders approval to go ahead with the scheme.

An application was received to convert number 58 Boldmere Road, previously F. C. Wareham's Old Warwick Lending Library, into a Greek take-away. It was refused by the Planning Committee who said it would adversely affect the neighbours. They also pointed out there were already three take-aways in the area and, if approved, would mean another break in shopping frontages in Boldmere Road. In spite of their refusal on this occasion, number 58 Boldmere Road has become a Chinese take-away under the name of *The House of Mr Li.*

SMALL TRADERS GIVE VARIETY TO THE AREA

Banks, building societies, chemists, multiple and chain stores in the High Streets of most towns create a very familiar look about them with the same shop frontages. So it is always sad when a small trader who has served the community for a very long time takes a well-earned retirement and there is no other member of the family to carry on the business.

80 Boldmere Road, circa 1930s, now incorporated into John Frost's.

THE OLDEST BUSINESS IN BOLDMERE?

One of the oldest businesses still trading in Boldmere is Allsops the family butchers at 29 Boldmere Road. Established in 1897 at 282 Boldmere Road, the business has been run by the Allsop family for three generations. Guy Allsop, the present owner continues the tradition of quality and service that has carried them through a century.

Another long established business is Bayliss the Bathroom and plumbing business in Gate Lane who were established in 1929.

Frosts — Boldmeres mini-department store recently celebrated its sixty years in business. Originally a small chemists shop it has expanded and extended over the years and now offers a wide range of general goods including Greetings Cards, Photography, Fancy Goods, Newspapers and Perfumes within a floor area of several thousand square feet.

OLD FAVOURITES GO

A letter published in the *Sutton News* in September 1990 from Mrs Ida Hillman, a Boldmere resident, drew attention to such a situation. She referred

John Frosts, 84 Boldmere Road, circa 1954.

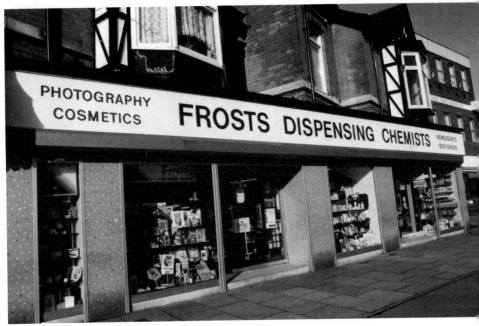

John Frost in 1994 now occupies 82 and 84 Boldmere Road.

to two old established businesses closing down. Firstly, that of Norman Pearson, Radio, Television and Electrical shop, number 18 Boldmere Road, which she remembered from her pre-war childhood.

She remembered as a child her parents speaking with sadness of the death of Norman Pearson, the young man who had opened the shop. The owner, Mrs Carter, known to everyone as Esther, was then a young assistant in the shop, who with her husband took over the business but retained the original name. She reminisced on the tremendous service Mrs Carter, her husband and staff had given the customers.

Where could we have got those much loved, well worn electrical gadgets mended? No matter how old and dilapidated the articles were, they would have a go and 99 times out of a 100 were successful in returning them to their owners in perfect working order Where else do you go and have the light bulb tested before it is handed to you?

Secondly, **Hilda Walker,** *as our wool and baby-wear shop owned by Olive Watkins was called. Even if you didn't want to purchase anything there was always a welcome in her shop. She too is taking a well-earned retirement."*

Having reached the year 1990 and a new decade Boldmere continues to face up to the demands of a modern age. Many old established businesses have

*An enlarged detail of the
name plaque on the house
in the main photograph.*

*Mrs Elizabeth Allen outside her
Victorian villa in Boldmere Road,
almost opposite Redacre Road,
taken at the turn of the century.*

... And as it is today.

Shops on corner of Redacre Road and Boldmere Road, c.1945. Note number 56 currently occupied by Thomas & Jones, watch repairers, was still a house.

gone to be replaced by new trades unfamiliar to our predecessors. Some of the old original buildings having served their purpose have been demolished and new modern looking structures have gone in their place.

NEW FACES ARRIVE

A selection of new businesses appeared in the local press in December 1990, advertising Christmas cards, gifts and a variety of services. Our great-grandparents would have had no idea what a hi-fi or television was, but that is what *Amadeus* at number 10 Boldmere Road was offering for sale, having taken over the premises from Chris. C. Moore, ironmonger, where you were able to purchase single items, instead of a packet, as one has to today.

Glovers Ceramics, an established family business in Gate Lane, provided a useful service for the family out shopping, by installing a new fully-equipped play area where children could play in safety while mom and dad could browse around.

Both ends of Boldmere are well appointed with places to eat, having several take-aways offering English, Indian and Chinese food, plus an assortment of tea shops for light refreshments, grills etc.

In addition there are a number of licenced restaurants and pubs giving a very wide choice of sit down meals and of course pub food.

When Mason Sorrel, Ladies Hairdresser, left 98 Boldmere Road, opposite the present *Harvester,* they were succeeded by *Miscellany,* described as an Aladdin's cave of goodies, selling cane furniture for all rooms in the house, pottery dinner services and a whole range of goods.

H. L. Groves, 86 Boldmere Road, was followed by *Private Collection,* selling a wide selection of fascinating carved wooden items: wooden chests, picture frames, collector dolls and soft furnishings.

Vogue, with ladies fashions from all over the Continent occupy 57-59 Boldmere Road. Their address was once given as 55 Boldmere Road. Many people still remember number 57 as the MEB and number 59 as Bayliss & Co Ltd., builders merchants.

Fleetwoods Delicatessen, 51-53 Boldmere Road, established for 26 years specialises in home made bread, cakes, meats, quiches and 60 different cheeses.

For those interested in local history, whether they be reading it up or perhaps requiring their manuscripts to be published, there can be no better place locally than at 44 Boldmere Road, the home of *Westwood Press*, who have published a wide variety of local history books, which in recent years has established them as specialists in that field. They do, however, print a considerable variety of other items: invoices, wedding stationery; in fact almost anything the customer may require.

Shops in Boldmere Road, between Redacre Road and Jockey Road.

At the further end of Boldmere, known to residents as Little Boldmere, is the *Cork and Bottle* Wine Bar at 363 Boldmere Road, which offers wines, spirits and meals

The list of shops and businesses is far too long to print, but the best place to find out who is where in Boldmere is the current edition of the *Thompson Directory*. The above is a selection taken from the 1990 Christmas Advertisements.

IT CAME FROM ON HIGH

A year later, in March 1991, a Boldmere couple, David and Frances Batts of Halton Road, were stunned by bangs which shook the House to its foundations. They thought a crash had occurred outside their home and went out to investigate only to find all was perfectly normal.

The next morning Mr Batts was returning home from the newsagents when he saw a gaping hole in his roof. Apparently the right hand side undercarriage fairing of a Trans-European Boeing 737 had fallen from the aircraft as it was preparing to land at Birmingham International Airport and had crashed through the roof and then shot back out into the garden. Another few inches and it could have come through the ceiling and there is no doubt it could have killed someone. Their house is on the flight path to Birmingham International Airport and Mr Batts said that they had become used to the noise of aircraft passing overhead, but this incident had made them feel nervous.

ROBERT MAXWELL CONNECTIONS

Boldmere received the interest of the National Press in 1991 when Robert Maxwell, owner of the *Daily Mirror* and other newspapers, fell overboard with a massive heart attack from his private luxury yacht just off the Canary Isles. Many stories were written about him after his death including one concerning a Boldmere woman.

In 1940 Maxwell had come to Britain from Czechoslovakia and was interned in an internment camp at Westwood Coppice, Sutton Park. He wished to fight for Britain against the Germans, but was unable to speak English, so he enlisted the assistance of a Boldmere lady to teach him to speak English, which he accomplished in six weeks.

BOLDMERE'S INDUSTRIAL ESTATE

A passageway between *Fleetwoods Delicatessen* and *Lasting Impressions* formerly *Boldmere Florists* is Union Drive, which leads to a little known industrial estate. On the estate can be found *Powelectrics Ltd.*, a family run business, started by Henry Powell in 1973, which is a distributor for a number of companies manufacturing electronic components for the automation industry and counts amongst its customers some of the country's leading companies.

The industrial estate consists of factories and offices which during the current recession has seen a regular turnover of occupiers. These together with the long established businesses and workshops in the better known Gate Lane comprise a substantial commercial element in the Boldmere community.

Gate Lane, off Boldmere Road

In November 1991 Boldmere Library re-opened to the public after being closed for some weeks for renovation and alteration. The revamped library boasted a refurbished interior, including a new shelving system. A new computer system was being installed which would give the library immediate access to over one million books in stock.

DRAINAGE THE FINAL SOLUTION?

From the time Boldmere started to develop in the mid 1800s it has always had problems over disposal of its waste water and sewerage and many attempts to resolve the situation have been tried. However, in 1992, starting at the traffic lights at the Boldmere Road junction new sewerage pipes were laid right up Jockey Road to the top near the *Beggars Bush Inn*.

This took about twelve months to complete. Then in 1993 a start was made at the Chester Road entrance to Boldmere Road, which should solve the problem of waste water and sewerage disposal in Boldmere Road.

The final stages of waste water and sewerage disposal should be completed in 1994 when new pipes will be laid all along Monmouth Drive and an overflow tank constructed to avoid water and raw sewage being diverted into *Powells Pool* and subsequently the River Tame via the Ebrook.

Boldmere Today — a Thriving Community

Over the past 150 years Boldmere has grown from a rural community with its quaint country pubs to a modern, thriving, bustling district. The coming of the railway in 1862 gave impetus to its growth providing a quick means of transport for the commuter to Birmingham, who was encouraged to set down his roots here.

Its housing estates were complimented by its schools, churches and services, such as banks, post offices, chemists and various good quality shops concentrated at both ends of Boldmere Road. By the 1930s most of the building land had been used up and some of the older properties were in the 1960s beginning to be replaced by more modern buildings.

Today the present residents of Boldmere have all the facilities they require at hand, or nearby in Sutton or Birmingham, whilst just down the road on their doorstep they have access to one of the country's well-known recreational beauty spots, and Sutton Coldfield's "Jewel in the Crown" — those 2400 acres called Sutton Park.

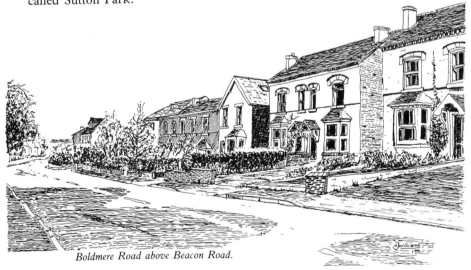

Boldmere Road above Beacon Road.

A Chronological History of Boldmere

1528	Three farms: Old Park Farm, Booths Farm and Stonehouse Farms in existence.
1610	Speed's Map shows "Cofeld Wast" — which includes Boldmere yet to be named.
1679	Called the Coldfield: Some land owned John Allport, Gent.
1729	London silk dyer murdered on Chester Road. Edward Allport hung on Gibbet Hill.
1700s	Stonehouse Farm in existence (Tom Porter reported a track across land, now covered by pool). Also, Old Park Farm and Booths Farm.
1730	Sir Thomas Holte builds dam and creates pool of over 40 acres — later known as Powell's Pool.
1733	John Wyatt, inventor, experiments with cotton spinning in a shed on the dam.
1750s	William Powell working rolling mill at the dam on "Powells Pool".
1783	February: William Hutton visits Sutton. Encounters Bowens Pool. Approaches from the Coldfield.
1802	Erdington enclosures map shows "Bowmere" Lake spanning Chester Road (turnpike).
1810	Lake (Bowmore) now called "Baldmoore"
1824	Inclosure Award. The Coldfield divided up and enclosed.
1827	(Powell's) Pool called New Forge Pool on map.
1830	Francis Parkes involved with the mill at Powell's Pool.
1839	John Buggins, farmer, sold land on which St Nicholas Chapel built.
1840	Roman Catholic Chapel of St Nicholas built by Bishop Wiseman on the Coldfield (Boldmere Road). Seated 50 people and served from Erdington and New Oscott College.
1841	William Goodwin, Landlord of Bush Inn.
1844	Stonehouse on bank of Powell's Pool built by Francis Parkes.
1845	Thomas Parkes at mill and forge.
1848	The Reverend Jas. Moore, School House.
1848	Francis Parkes' new partner is John Alliban.
1848	Chester Road Pool now called "Baldmoor" Lake (see 1810).
1848	School for Girls and Infants built in Boldmere Road.
1848	William Coley, beer house, the Coldfield (he the owner).
1850s	Occupier of Powell's Pool, John Buggins.
1850	Grove Cottage first recorded.
1853	The Reverend Bedford forms committee to build a Church in Boldmere.
1855	Thirty men and boys employed at Spade Mill.
1855	Owner of mill and pool, Lord Somerville.
1856/7	St Michael's Church built at Boldmere. Cost: £2,663 (minus steeple). Stone laid in 1856 by Countess of Bradford. First Vicar: Rev. E. H. Kittoe.
1856	Parochial valuation — names — "The Coldfield" also "Baldmoor" Lake.
1857	Map shows Baldmoor Lane, but does not show its name.

1858	New ecclesiastical parish of "Boldmere" formed.
1860	Birmingham Sutton Railway line contracts signed.
1861	Names— Coldfield, Bolemere and Bolemere Lake recorded.
1862	Sutton Railway Line opened 2nd June 1862.
1864	Two almshouses (to be) built in Boldmere.
1867	James Palmer and George Hodgkinson of mill — bankrupt (Spade Mill).
1871	Poor Rate Book spellings — Baldmoore and Balemore.
1871	John Burt, occupier of Powell's Pool.
1871	Extension to St Michael's Church. £1,320 raised by public subscription.
1871	Spire added to St Michael's Church.
1876	Gas installed in St Michael's Church.
1882	(Map) Stonehouse Road named Park Lane (also 1886 map).
1883	Boldmere St Michael's Football Team formed from Bible Class.
1886	Map shows name "Boldmere" Road.
1886	Boldmere Swimming Club's first annual water carnival at Powell's Pool.
1889	Hubert A. Done — Cold Steel Roller and Steam Boat Proprietor.
1890	Steamboat "Foam" on Powell's Pool.
1890	Pool known as "Powell's" or "Spade Mill Pool".
1900	Name *Grove Cottage* first mentioned — recorded in *Sutton Coldfield/Erdington Directory*.
1900	Powell's Pool Co Ltd, Steel Rollers, Stonehouse Mill.
1901	New Infants' School built in Boldmere Road.
1901	Stonehouse Road widened. Park gates at Boldmere replaced.
1904	United Reformed Church built in Britwell Road.
1904 & 1921	Park Lane (ie Stonehouse Road) now on map as part of Boldmere Road.
1912	Mr Marston remarked on the astonishing growth of Boldmere.
1912	Permission to run single decker buses through Sutton Coldfield.
1912	Lodge House built at Boldmere entrance to Sutton Park. Cost £425.
1913	Chester Road Baptist Church built.
1914	Firm — John E. Mapplebeck rolls brass strip for War effort.
1914	Electric lights switched on in St Michael's Church (mains extension to Boldmere completed).
1918	William Harrison, builder, killed by water wheel in October 1918. Mill later empty and derelict.
1925	Highbury Little Theatre founded.
1929-30	Monmouth Drive cut.
1930s	Part of mill roof collapsed. Building unsafe.
1933	Chester Road Cricket Club, Church Road (later Boldmere F.C. Ground).
1935	Boldmere Minicipal Golf Course opened. Arthur Rickets first professional.
1935	Houses for sale corner Britwell and Highbridge Roads. Cost £575.
1936	Mill demolished.
1937	Powell's Pool purchased by Corporation. Becomes part of Sutton Coldfield.

1938	Name "Stonehouse" Road shown on 1938 map (but only between the Park gate and Monmouth Drive). Also "Monmouth Drive" now appears.
1938	Boldmere Infant, Junior and Senior Schools built.
1938	Agreement to allow double decker Midland Red buses to run through Sutton in the following year, 1939.
1938	Boldmere St Michael's Football Club new club house opened.
1940s	Bomb dropped behind houses in Stonehouse Road. Bomb dropped in Jockey Road.
1942	Curtain up for first time at Highbury Little Theatre.
1940s	Boldmere Football Club ground occupied by A.F.S.
1940s	Robert Maxwell (future owner of the *Daily Mirror*) interned in Czechoslovakian Camp at Westwood Coppice, Sutton Park. Boldmere woman teaches him to speak English.
1946	Boldmere Football Club ground de-requisitioned.
1940	Original Girls' and Infants School (unused as school) used as ambulance station.
1950s	Stonehouse Farm demolished.
1953	New Roman Catholic Church, Boldmere opened 6th March 1953.
1954	Family of five evicted from 14' x 7' shed behind 395 Jockey Road.
1954	Two new roads: Denholm Road and Stirling Road.
1955	Flooding in Britwell Road.
1957	World Jubilee Scout Jamboree, Sutton Park.
1960	Boldmere Branch Library opened.
1960	Sutton's first high rise flats built in Boldmere.
1964	Boldmere traffic island replaced by traffic signals.
1964	Somerville Estate of 45 acres being developed.
1964	St Michael's Church gutted by fire.
1965	56 acres of farmland at Princess Alice sold off for £685,000
1967	Jockey Road widened. 150 houses lose part of their gardens.
1967	Rebuilt St Michael's Church consecrated.
1972	Arsonist at large in Sutton.
1975	Baby abandoned in telephone box.
1976	Trouble at spinney to stop football.
1976	Boldmere becomes smokeless zone.
1978	Gate Lane gulley closed off to stop vandals.
1982	Sheffield Road becomes one way street.
1983	More trouble at Spinney: BMX bike gangs.
1991	Aircraft wheel fairing crashes through house roof, Halton Road.
1992	New sewers laid, Jockey Road.
1993	New sewers laid, Boldmere Road.
1994	New sewers laid along Monmouth Drive.

Index

Sources

(all in Sutton Coldfield Local History Library)

Maps: Speed 1610: Greenwood 1820: Corn Rent 1824: OS 1834: OS 1850: OS 1857.

Plan of the Parish 1857: Sales Catalogue C1880: OS 1882: 1886: 1904: 21:38

Erdington Enclosures Award 1802 — 1810: Map OS 1817

Map: Where bombs fell in Sutton Coldfield 1939-45.

History & Topography of Warwickshire 1830.

National Commercial Directory. Pigot: 1835

History, Gazeteer and Directory of Warwickshire: White. 1850

Burgess Role Borough of Sutton Coldfield, Boldmere Ward: 1886: 1890.

Kellys Directory: 1892/5: 1896: 1900: 1904: 1908: 1912: 1916: 1924: 1940.

Sutton Coldfield Newspaper cuttings: 1872-1897: 1890-1930: 1892-1979: 1910-1915: 1938-1944: 1888-1975: 1884-1983:

Birmingham Post 1972

Programme, Boldmere Special Entertainment: 1884

A Sutton Coldfield Source Book. 3 volumes. Fentiman. OSH 97.

Sutton News: 1991: 10.03.67: 1989

Interview with Miss Ogden 1991

Popular Guide to Sutton Park: Sidwell and Durrant 1890.

Poor Rate Book 1845: 1848: 1855: 1861: 1871.

History of Sutton Coldfield, W. K. Riland-Bedford 1891.

A Commemorative History of Sutton Coldfield: Douglas V. Jones 1973.

Commercial Directory and Gazeteer of Warwickshire: Morris 1866.

Plans and Papers concerning the tithe rents in Sutton Coldfield 1786-1903.

Post Office Directory of Warwickshire, Staffs and Worcestershire: 1864.

Census: 1861: 1851: 1841.

Minutes of the Warden and Society 1852.

Sutton Coldfield Register of Electors 1851-2.

Borough of Sutton Coldfield Education Minutes 1851-1868.

School Attendance Committee 1891.

A History of Oscott College, J. H. Thompson.

Town School, Sutton Coldfield, Log Book 1826-1904.

Inclosure Award, Schedule of Allotments 1850.

History of Birmingham: William Hutton.

Sutton Coldfield and District Directory 1900, 1901-2.

Boldmere Swimming Club, Programme.

Report of the Park and Estates Committee 1913: 1941-1957.

Birmingham Evening Mail 1933: 1953: 1972: 1981: 1983.

Sutton Coldfield Magazine: 1963.

Borough of Sutton Coldfield, Highways Committee 1928-9.

Boldmere Golf Club Official Handbook

Correspondence and Deed of Gift re Spinney 1986

John Wyatt, Master Carpenter & Inventor AD 1700-1766, London 1855.

Westwood Press Publications

THE ROYAL TOWN of SUTTON COLDFIELD
A Commemorative History
by Douglas V. Jones

Running to 208 pages and covering the period from Saxon times up till 1974, when the Royal Town of Sutton Coldfield was amalgamated with Birmingham, this is a warm human story of local people, events and landmarks.

SUTTON COLDFIELD 1974-1984 The Story of a Decade
The Modern sequel to the History of Sutton
by Douglas V. Jones

A lavishly illustrated Chronicle which recalls the many changes to the face of Sutton since its merger with Birmingham, together with a Pictorial Supplement, *Sutton in 1984.*

SUTTON PARK, Its History and Wildlife
by Douglas V. Jones

Profusely illustrated with a wide selection of old and new pictures most of which have not previously been published, complete with centrefold map, and detailed with three interesting walks short enough for the casual walker to take at leisure.

STEAMING UP TO SUTTON How the Birmingham to Sutton
Coldfield Railway Line was built in 1862
written by Roger Lea

Every day thousands travel on the railway line between Sutton and Birmingham, without giving much thought to its origins and history. This is the fascinating story.

THE STORY OF ERDINGTON
From Sleepy Hamlet to Thriving Suburb
by Douglas V. Jones

Tracing the history of Erdington from earliest times, through the ages up to the late twentieth century. With some ninety-eight illustrations including a period map circa 1880.

MEMORIES OF A TWENTIES CHILD
by Douglas V. Jones

A nostalgic trip into one man's childhood and youth during the years between the wars. The book is a profusely illustrated reminder of the age of steam, gas-lamps, crystal-sets and tramcars.

DURATION MAN 1939-46, My War
by Douglas V. Jones

An enthralling sequal to "Memories of a Twenties Child"

This is the story of some of those who fought the good fight against red tape, boredom and gloom in places where all three were often present. If from time to time it may appear that soldiering is a mug's game, then the reader must draw his own conclusions. 144 pages, fully illustrated.

THE BOOK OF BRUM or Mekya Selfa Tum
by Ray Tennant

Random thoughts on the dialect and accent of the Second City (Brumslang) with a glossary of the most common expressions plus Brumodes, Brumverse and Brumericks with a little more serious verse. Brilliantly illustrated with appropriate cartoons by Jim Lyndon.

Last Tram Down the Village and Other Memories of
YESTERDAY'S BIRMINGHAM
by Ray Tennant

Although all the places written about are centred in or very near to Birmingham it will, hopefully, be of interest to people who live in other cities since many of the memories could be shared and appreciated by anyone who lived through the traumatic years of the thirties and forties.

The Second BOOK OF BRUM Aware Din Urea
by Ray Tennant

Further thoughts on the dialect and accent of Birmingham with a glossary containing many sayings of historical interest plus a little more verse and cartoons by Lyndon. Many expressions from the past are included in this Second Book of Brum.